The Cosmos of the Soul II

Messages

Michele Doucette

The Cosmos of the Soul II: Messages

ISBN 978-1-935786-74-0

Printed in the United States of America by

St. Clair Publications

PO Box 726

McMinnville, TN   37111-0726

http://stclairpublications.com/

Table of Contents

Author's Note

In 2011, <u>The Cosmos of the Soul: A Spiritual Biography</u> was published.

The life story of every individual is unique; as such, each deserves to be treasured, to be acknowledged, to be remembered.

In the words of author Susan Wittig Albert ... *The spiritual path represents the Process of Becoming whereby the soul remembers itself and the soul discovers its true identity as spirit.*

We now have the second installation, namely, <u>The Cosmos of the Soul II: Messages</u>, a book of reflective messages, and related websites, divided into units of study.

In an email dated December 29, 2013, Cyndi Krupp shares that ......

[1] 2012 was a year of cocooning and waiting.

[2] 2013 was about chaos and shifting; learning how to ride out the storm.

[3] 2014 is the year we all get to reap the harvest of what we have planted.

The question now becomes, what have *you* taken the time to plant?

While I do not believe in a doomsday scenario, I very much resonate with what has been referred to as the Shift of the Ages. [1]

What is this shift that we are all feeling? [2] [3]

[1] It is a shift in how we think.

[2] It is a shift in how we live.

---

[1] http://www.shiftoftheages.com/
[2] Ibid.
[3] http://www.zengardner.com/shift/

[3] It is a growing awareness of this majestic planet.

[4] It is a growing awareness in who we are as a people.

[5] It is a time of awakening.

[6] It is a remarkable period in the history of this planet.

Choices to be made by all, these choices are more important now than ever before.

We are one family.

We have but one home.

You are your own Nelson Mandela.

You are your own Mahatma Gandhi.

You are your own Buddha.

You are your own Christ.

2012 and Earth Activations [4]

2012: Not the End of the World says oldest Mayan Calendar [5][6][7][8][9]

2012: What's The Real Truth? [10]

All About 2012 [11]

An Explanation about the Mayans and 2012 [12]

_____

[4] http://www.coasttocoastam.com/shows/2012/11/22
[5] http://www.livescience.com/20218-apocalypse-oldest-mayan-calendar.html
[6] http://www.ibtimes.com/oldest-mayan-calendar-unearthed-guatemala-slams-2012-doomsday-myth-photos-video-697981
[7] http://digitaljournal.com/article/324725
[8] http://www.sciencemag.org/content/336/6082/714
[9] http://news.nationalgeographic.com/news/2012/05/120510-maya-2012-doomsday-calendar-end-of-world-science/?source=hp_dl1_news_maya20120510
[10] http://jhaines6.wordpress.com/2012/07/08/red-ice-radio-drunvalo-melchizedek-mayan-ouroboros-2012-mayan-calendar/
[11] http://www.13moon.com/prophecy%20page.htm#nav4
[12] http://www.crawford2000.co.uk/mayan-calendar-2012-prophecies.htm

Consciousness Videos [13]

Drunvalo Melchizedek School of Remembering [14]

Hopi Elders Say Earth Changes Are Upon Us [15]

The Mayan Calendar, Part 1 [16]

The Mayan Calendar, Part 2 [17]

The Mayan Countdown to 2012 [18]

_____

[13] http://www.mysticmamma.com/consciousness-videos/
[14] http://www.drunvalo.net/
[15]

http://kryon.com/inspiritmag/articles/HopiPredictions_06/HopiPredictions.html
[16] http://www.crawford2000.co.uk/maya-2012-predictions-2012-prophecy.htm
[17] http://www.crawford2000.co.uk/maya-2012-predictions-2012-prophecy-2.htm
[18] http://www.crawford2000.co.uk/maya-2012-prophecy-count-.htm

The Mayan Ouroboros: The Cosmic Cycles Come Full Circle [19]

The Untold Positive Side of the Mayan Prophecies [20]

The Miracle of the Breath

Take a few moments to contemplate the wonder of breathing; in and out, in and out, in and out. It is imperative that we take the time to truly appreciate the first miracle of life, all courtesy of the power of the breath.

In truth, we must become more mindful of this exquisite gift, a gift beyond measure, a gift that many of us have a tendency to take completely for granted.

Without attempting to achieve transcended awareness, one can experience a change in consciousness when they take five to ten minutes, per day, to concentrate solely on the process of breathing.

Find a comfortable place where you shall not be disturbed.

Feel free to listen to a musical selection that relaxes you, but without taking your focus away from the breathing exercise.

Sitting with a straight back, take a deep breath, slowly and naturally, expanding the diaphragm as you fill your lungs to capacity. Hold the breath for a count of ten before releasing.

Once again, take a deep breath, hold for a count of ten and then release.

Upon completion, you will find yourself in a different state of mind; what a wonderful way to begin and/or end each day.

In taking this to another level, Adrian Cooper, author of a book called <u>Our Ultimate Reality: Life, the Universe, and the Destiny of Mankind</u>, manages a website whereby one can subscribe to a weekly newsletter.

In was in the May 16, 2010 installment located at http://www.ourultimatereality.com/newsletters/160510.pdf whereby he took the time to address the issue of right breathing, stating that most people are not aware that the process of breathing has significance far beyond merely supplying the physical body with ample oxygen.

There are three fundamental ways in which we breathe:

[1] from the neck and shoulders (the most shallow form of breathing)

[2] from the chest (the way most healthy people breathe)

[3] from the solar plexus (the most profound and spiritual way of breathing).

In keeping with the Yogi's of India, the Monks of Tibet, and the Martial Arts Masters of Japan, Cooper shares that their powers come from one fundamental purpose: to unite with and express Source, a process that is very much associated with right breathing.

While Olympic athletes know the importance of controlled breathing, few practice right breathing.

While those who meditate know the importance of deep relaxation, there are very few who actually practice right breathing.

In summation, right breathing, according to Cooper, is the source of all physical, mental and spiritual power.

Situated just below the navel (belly button) is the solar plexus.

Cooper shares that ... *just as the navel is our point of connection with the Source of Life in the Womb through which we are nourished and sustained by the Mother, the corresponding Solar Plexus Chakra is our point of Connection with the Womb of the Universe from and through which we are expressed: the Source of All That Is,* meaning that right breathing serves to facilitate the flow of Universal life energy when the solar plexus chakra has been appropriately developed.

It is imperative, then, that we learn to make the solar plexus the focus center of our breathing.

Cooper shares the directions to right breathing.

1. Inhale for as long and as deeply as you can in through your nose, with your mouth closed.

Ensure that this inhalation is long, smooth and progressive. Continue this inhalation until you feel your lungs are as full as possible without discomfort.

2. Now press that breath down to your abdomen, the location of your navel, really feeling your abdominal region expanding with the pressure as much as you can without feeling excessive discomfort.

You should feel this breath now firmly centered in the region of your navel, knowing this to be true.

3. With your centre of focus remaining on the breath in your abdominal area, part your lips slightly and exhale very slowly through your mouth, always feeling and knowing that you are exhaling from the abdominal area where your mind is focused.

This slow release of breath should last at least 10 seconds, 15 seconds is better.

While a person may feel discomfort at first, Cooper further advises one to persevere in the knowledge that they will soon become used to this right breathing until it becomes natural.

He also shares that you may feel various sensations due to the much greater Universal life energy flow.

It is important that you treat these as positive confirmations of success.

―――――――――✕―――――――――

Breath Mastery [21]

Miracles of the Qur'an [22]

The Breath of Life [23]

The Miracle of Spiritual Breathing [24]

The Miracle of the Breath [25] [26] [27] [28]

―――――――――――

[21] http://www.breathmastery.com/
[22] http://www.miraclesofthequran.com/scientific_59.html
[23] http://www.breath.org/
[24] http://www.selfgrowth.com/articles/the-miracle-of-spiritual-breathing
[25] http://www.dailyom.com/library/000/001/000001129.html
[26] http://www.naturalhealthweb.com/articles/cperkins1.html
[27] http://www.realyoga.org/weekly-lecture.php?mode=archive&id=85
[28] http://deepyogablog.com/2013/01/11/the-miracle-of-breath/

Message 1

A SPIRITUAL BEING

I know that I am a spiritual being living a human experience, as per Pierre Teilhard de Chardin. I also know that I am here to live a purpose filled life. How, then, does one go about shedding the unnecessary weights of self-doubt and insecurity that continue to surface from time to time?

First and foremost, I *never* make New Year's resolutions; instead, I prefer that each day continue to be a journey from mindlessness to mindfulness.

To my way of thinking, mindlessness refers to the world of physical bodies, brains and separation thinking (of the Ego); a world whereby we either operate on autopilot, perform in a mechanical (rote) fashion (because we are just going through the motions), or simply do not pay attention.

It is most unfortunate that very few people actually realize the extent to which they live a mindless life.

Mindfulness, on the other hand, refers to recognizing that this existence is but a dream, and, as the dreamer of the dream, you can change the source of the dream from the thought system of separation (of the Ego) to the thought system of forgiveness and healing (of the Heart) so that you can find the peace, the truth, the wisdom, that exists within.

So, too, is mindfulness about fully experiencing the present moment; taking in all that is around us in a non-judgmental way.

Mindfulness enables one to realize that they have a role to play, as a part of a greater whole, in the tapestry of life that we have taken the time to weave together.

Anger is never justified because anger says that I am separate, which is exactly what the Ego wants me to believe.

Once this mindfulness and peace has been experienced, anger is no longer justified because forgiveness and healing reminds me that we are all One.

In accordance with this belief, forgiveness and healing must always begin with me.

In the words of Jack Layton ... *My friends, love is better than anger, hope is better than fear, optimism is better than despair; so let us be loving, hopeful and optimistic, and we will change the world.*

PIERRE TEILHARD DE CHARDIN

American Teilhard Association (ATA) [29]

Association des Amis de Pierre Teilhard de Chardin [30]

---

[29] http://www.teilharddechardin.org/
[30] http://www.teilhard.fr/

Cosmogenesis and Consciousness [31]

Religion, Science and Mysticism in Pierre Teilhard de Chardin [32]

Teilhard for Beginners [33]

The British Teilhard Association [34]

The Future of Man by Pierre Teilhard de Chardin [35]

The Teilhard de Chardin Project [36]

MINDFULNESS

Benefits of Mindfulness [37]

---

[31] http://www.huffingtonpost.com/dave-pruett/cosmogenesis-and-consciou_b_4084855.html

[32] http://www.earthlight.org/essay39_king.html

[33] http://www.teilhardforbeginners.com/

[34] http://www.teilhard.org.uk/

[35] https://archive.org/details/TheFutureOfMan

[36] http://www.teilhardproject.com/

[37] http://www.helpguide.org/harvard/mindfulness.htm

Buddhism: Miracle of Mindfulness [38]

Greater Good Science Centre [39]

Guided Audio Mindfulness Exercises [40]

Mindfulness [41] [42]

Mindfulness Everyday [43]

Mindfulness Exercises [44]

---

[38]

http://www.lifepositive.com/Spirit/Buddhism/Miracle_Mind
fulness.asp

[39]

http://greatergood.berkeley.edu/topic/mindfulness/definition

[40] http://www.mindfulschools.org/about-
mindfulness/mindfulness-exercises/?gclid=CPuK37j-
1bsCFYtQOgodvy0AFQ

[41] http://blogs.theprovince.com/tag/mindfulness/

[42]

http://www.vipassana.com/meditation/mindfulness_in_plain
_english_15.php

[43] http://www.mindfulnesseveryday.com/

[44] http://youth.anxietybc.com/mindfulness-exercises

Mindfulness: Finding Peace in a Frantic World [45]

Mindfulness Research [46]

Mindfulness Without Borders [47]

Sati [48]

The Mindfulness Bell [49]

The Mindfulness Institute [50]

------

[45] http://franticworld.com/

[46] http://www.huffingtonpost.com/news/gps-mindfulness-research/

[47] http://mindfulnesswithoutborders.org/

[48] http://dharma.ncf.ca/introduction/instructions/sati.html

[49] http://www.iamhome.org/index.php

[50] http://www.mindfulnessbasedlearning.com/Home.aspx

Message 2

I AM A CREATOR

I *create* what I speak (think about, believe, act upon).

Negative thoughts create negative beliefs; these beliefs prevent me from moving forward.

My subconscious creates what I believe. In a nutshell, this means that I must learn to ......

[1] eliminate all feelings of doubt, fear and self-sabotage.

[2] replace all negative thoughts with those that serve only to empower me (thereby rendering the negative thoughts completely powerless).

[3] give my subconscious new beliefs (new instructions) upon which to act.

[4] realize that I *am* good enough.

Easier said than done, you *can* control that which you focus on.

Living the human experience, there are times when I take one step forward and two steps back (as the saying goes); something that everyone can relate to.

While this experience can be a most arduous one, I *refuse* to be a defeatist.

The more present I am in the moment, the less negativity (doubt, uncertainty, fear of failure, fear of being wrong, disempowering self-talk, lack of self-belief, shame, poor focus, comparing yourself to others, procrastination, self-sabotage, anxiety, panic, worry, depression, utter helplessness) I actually experience.

It is important that I listen to my self-talk in order to better identify the problem.

It is important that I commit to change.

It is important that I am willing to grow.

It is important that I focus on my strengths.

It is important that I stop replaying, and reliving, past scenarios in my mind's eye.

It is important that I embrace opportunities when they arise.

It is important that I watch my words because my words create my world.

It is important that I continue to move forward.

It is important that I am willing to heal.

It is important that I embrace feelings of calm, peace, happiness and clarity.

It is imperative that I work with as many different techniques as I can to negate all negative thoughts; positive thoughts always lead to positive living.

I must take the time to nurture my mind with positive feedback.

When I am able to eliminate the negative thinking and limiting beliefs, so that my subconscious mind completely absorbs the new positive thoughts (and beliefs), empowering changes become evident.

The next few chapters that follow outline some of the specific mediums and techniques that I have used, and am continuing to use, all in an effort to reconfigure my subconscious mind.

There is also an end chapter entitled Affiliate Links; this is where I outline the programs that I have purchased, and utilized, and am now willing to endorse as an affiliate.

Affirmation Method

Affirmations are personal statements written in both positive and present tense terms; the more emotion one evokes upon reciting affirmations aloud, the more powerful they become.

Affirmations are positive statements, or directions, you state to yourself, all in an effort to bring about necessary changes in your subconscious behavior patterns (to whatever you will them to be).

For affirmations to be effective, they must always be stated as positive, already accomplished, results.

Wording them in futuristic terms, such as [1] I will be, [2] I am going to be, or [3] I would like to be actually *prevents the changes from ever taking place* because we are always living in the now.

Therefore, *giving energy to the positive trait*, such as I am always Unselfishly Loving *always supersedes the negative*, (as in I will become Unselfishly Loving).

You need to *feel*, *mean* and *believe the words* as you say them, or the affirmation will not be an effective tool.

---

35 Affirmations That Will Change Your Life [51]

Affirmation List [52] [53]

Affirmation Station [54]

Affirmations: What They Are and How to Use Them to Create a Better Life [55]

---

[51] http://www.huffingtonpost.com/dr-carmen-harra/affirmations_b_3527028.html

[52] http://aplacefortheheart.co.uk/affirmations/affirmationlist/

[53] http://www.vitalaffirmations.com/affirmations.htm#.UvzF5jiPK1s

[54] http://www.affirmationstation.com/FREE-stuff_ep_28.html

[55] http://www.self-help-and-self-development.com/affirmations.html

Affirmations: Words with Power [56]

Daily Affirmation (Louise L. Hay) [57]

Examples of Positive Affirmations [58]

How to Write and Effective Affirmation [59]

Little Affirmations (Affirmations Publishing House) [60]

Mind Medicine (Affirmations Publishing House) [61]

Positive Affirmations: A Positive Thinking Technique For Change [62]

---

[56]

http://www.successconsciousness.com/books/affirmations_words_power.htm

[57] http://www.louisehay.com/affirmations/

[58]

http://www.essentiallifeskills.net/positiveaffirmations.html

[59] http://www.wikihow.com/Write-an-Effective-Affirmation

[60] http://www.affirmations.com.au/retail_default/little-affirmations/little-affirmations-range.html

[61] http://www.affirmations.com.au/retail_default/mind-medicine.html

[62] http://www.vitalaffirmations.com/

Power Affirmations: Power Positive Conditioning for Your Subconscious Mind (William H. Marshall) [63]

Refreshing Beliefs (1500 Affirmations) [64]

The A to Z of Affirmations [65]

The Only 100 Positive Affirmations You Will Ever Need [66]

Unlock The Secret To Using Affirmations [67]

Using Affirmations: Harnessing Positive Thinking [68]

------

[63] http://www.poweraffirmations.com/

[64] http://www.wisdomways.net/wisdom/RefreshingBeliefs/index.cfm?proAppName=wisdom

[65] http://thesoulagentblog.com/z-affirmations/

[66] http://www.prolificliving.com/100-positive-affirmations/

[67] http://www.thelawofattraction.com/want-to-feel-better-unlock-the-secret-to-using-affirmations/

[68] http://www.mindtools.com/pages/article/affirmations.htm

Afformation Method

Afformations (a new system devised by Noah St. John) are an important concept in the power of positive thinking.

As is the case with affirmations, afformations also focus on the positive; the key difference, however, is in asking a positive question rather than stating a positive statement.

Based on Noah St. John's book <u>The Secret Code of Success,</u> an afformation is the formulation of a question to empower your mind.

Rather than just stating something is true (as is the case with an affirmation), an afformation asks *why* it is true.

According to Noah St. John, our minds appreciate questions and are eager to search for answers.

He likens this process to an "automatic search function" in the brain, stating that sometimes it is not the answer(s) but the question(s) that makes the difference.

Knowing how powerful our thoughts can be, we repeat positive statements (affirmations) in an attempt to manifest our goals; many people have been quite successful with this approach.

For those who struggle in convincing their minds to believe these statements, afformations can be used to assist in the reframing of one's thoughts.

When you use an afformation to ask a question, it puts a different spin on things because *asking why causes you to stop, think and be in the moment.*

When asking why you attract love in your life, it might be because you are lovable; this, then, leads to further thoughts along the same line. You come to realize that not only do you deserve a loving partner, but you are also attractive, warm, compassionate, and ready to share your life with that someone special.

As with affirmations, the first step is to decide on what you want.

Once you have identified your goal, you need to formulate a question that assumes you already have what you want.

► Why am I so happy?

► Why am I so wealthy?

► Why is my life so full of joy?

► Why am I feeling abundantly powerful in my thoughts and actions?

► Why do I love and embrace my life?

► Why am I allowed to be, do and have all that I want in life?

Upon asking yourself these questions, you can see that an answer or solution is immediately sought; likewise, evidence to support the answer is also sought.

In essence, *the question becomes the answer.*

In taking notice of the answers that come to you, regarding the question(s) that you have posed, you will find that they tend to be positive. Should these thoughts lead to even more questions and positive thoughts, be sure to keep them going.

In asking yourself questions on a regular basis, you will denote that your mode of thinking changes; accordingly, your actions will also follow suit.

You will attract what you seek based on your thoughts and positive vibrations.

As Noah St. John tells us, the Afformation Method is not necessarily about finding the answers; instead, it is about asking the questions that will help you positively manifest your desires. The point of afformations, then, does not lie in finding the answer, but in asking better questions, more empowering questions.

With afformations, you take conscious control of the questions you ask.

Once you start gathering answers to your empowering questions, your internal beliefs begin to shift in a most powerful way.

This changes what the brain focuses on, which, quite naturally, changes how you think.

When you have been successful in changing how you think, your perspective has changed.

Once your perspective has changed, this brings about further change to your actions.

In changing your actions, you will have changed your life.

———————————❖———————————

Afformations FAQ [69]

Afformations: Discovering the Missing Piece to Abundance [70]

———————————

[69] http://www.iafform.com/faq.php
[70] http://omtimes.com/2013/11/afformations/

Afformations: More Powerful Than Positive Thinking [71]

How to Use Afformations to Change Your Life [72]

Huge List of Afformations [73]

<u>The Book of Afformations: Discovering the Missing Piece to Abundant Health, Wealth, Love, and Happiness</u> (Noah St. John) [74] [75]

Why I Use Afformations Every Morning [76]

---

[71] http://www.simplemindfulness.com/afformations/

[72] http://www.owningpink.com/blogs/owning-pink/how-to-use-afformations-to-change-your-life

[73] https://happyecho.com/afformations/

[74]

http://www.amazon.com/exec/obidos/ASIN/1401944140/portalsofspirit

[75]

http://www.amazon.ca/exec/obidos/ASIN/1401944140/portalsofsp01-20

[76] http://workwithpaulsnider.com/why-i-use-afformations-every-morning/

Brainwave Entrainment

As we know, everything around us exists at a certain frequency. Scientists and quantum physicists have told us that everything is made up of energy.

We measure every form of energy as a frequency; light has a frequency, smells have a frequency, even thoughts have a frequency.

You have thought patterns in different brainwave states, all of which can be measured in frequency.

In short, frequency makes up everything we can see and everything we cannot see.

If you can change a certain frequency, you can change everything.

While our mental state affects our brainwaves, the opposite is also true, meaning that *our brainwaves affect our mental state.*

This means *that we can actually control our mental state by controlling our brainwaves*; this is the key power behind Brainwave Entrainment.

Entrainment is a term "borrowed from physics which simply refers to the tendency for two vibrating bodies to lock into phase so that they vibrate in harmony. For example, one tuning fork, when struck and placed next to another tuning fork, will cause the second one to vibrate at the same frequency." [77]

If you were to take this same phenomenon and apply it to training the brain, as scientific studies have demonstrated, the possibilities are endless.

---

[77] Zelcovitch, Morry. (2009). *Brainwave Entrainment: What It Really Is And How It Can Benefit You* website accessed on November 6, 2010 at http://www.themorrymethod.com/brainwave-entrainment-really/

Much of what we encounter in our lives appears to emphasize the left hemisphere, thereby teaching us to become logical, analytical, cause and effect, beings who prefer established authority structures.

Many individuals need to learn how to engage the right hemisphere of the brain, thereby improving visual spatial skills, visual imagery, intuitiveness and memory.

We know that the brain operates on different levels, each with their own wavelength and frequency.

When the brain is "stimulated with pulsed sounds, the overall activity of the brain will respond to, and align with, these pulses. By selecting the desired rate, the brain can be naturally induced towards the selected brainwave state." [78]

In truth, its potential is limitless.

---

[78] Zelcovitch, Morry. (2009). *Brainwave Entrainment: What It Really Is And How It Can Benefit You* website accessed on November 6, 2010 at http://www.themorrymethod.com/brainwave-entrainment-really/

Here is an example of entrainment we can all relate to.

It is said that "the most powerful thing that can change your state, in an instant, is music. How many times were you in a certain state of mind and experiencing a certain disempowering emotion, but when you heard your favorite song, or upbeat music, you immediately started to feel very different?" [79]

⋯✕⋯

There are four brainwave pattern categories: Beta, Alpha, Theta and Delta.

Each of these brainwave patterns, associated with specific states, serve important functions.

Beta waves are quick waves of 13 to 30 times per second (Hz). Beta brainwave patterns are generated naturally when we are awake and alert.

---

[79] Tan, Enoch. *Brainwave Entrainment* article (March 2006).

Alpha waves exist between 8 and 12 Hz. Alpha waves usually occur during rest (when the eyes are closed), intellectual relaxation, deep relaxation, meditation or when calming the mind; the desired result of experienced meditators.

Theta waves exist between 4 and 7 Hz. This is commonly referred to as the dream or "twilight" state. Theta is associated with learning, memory, REM sleep and dreaming.

Memory development is enhanced while in this state. Likewise, memory is improved (especially long term memory) and access to unconscious material, reveries, free association, insights and creative ideas is increased.

Delta brainwave patterns usually occur when we are asleep. Delta waves, ranging from .5 to 3 Hz, are the slowest.

Research indicates that "brainwave entrainment stimulation in the Theta range appears to be a beneficial approach to accelerated learning" [80] while "applying brainwave entrainment in the Alpha range may result in benefits similarly found with Zen or Transcendental Meditation." [81]

Given the lifestyle that many of us are faced with on a day to day basis, "returning to a peaceful, mind/body way of being is becoming increasingly difficult to achieve and maintain for any period of time. This causes disease in the mind/body, which is why it is paramount for us to "relearn" or "retrain" ourselves to get back to these healthful and rejuvenating states." [82]

---

[80] Zelcovitch, Morry. (2009). *Brainwave Entrainment: What It Really Is And How It Can Benefit You* website accessed on November 6, 2010 at http://www.themorrymethod.com/brainwave-entrainment-really/
[81] Ibid.
[82] Ibid.

Experimentation and research on the effects and applications of Brainwave Entrainment are currently ongoing in governments and universities, as well as amongst health professionals and educators around the world.

---

6 Benefits of Brainwave Entrainment [83]

A Comprehensive Review of the Psychological Effects of Brainwave Entrainment [84]

A Scientific Overview [85]

Brainwave Entrainment [86]

---

[83] http://whatisbrainwaveentrainment.com/

[84] http://www.ncbi.nlm.nih.gov/pubmedhealth/PMH0027030/

[85] http://www.transparentcorp.com/products/np/entrainment.php

[86] http://www.huffingtonpost.com/david-mager/brain-wave-entrainment_b_4142898.html

The Essential Guide to Brainwave Entrainment and Binaural Beats [87]

The Morry Method™ (Cutting Edge Brainwave Entrainment) [88]

What Is Brainwave Entrainment? (article also features some special freebies) [89]

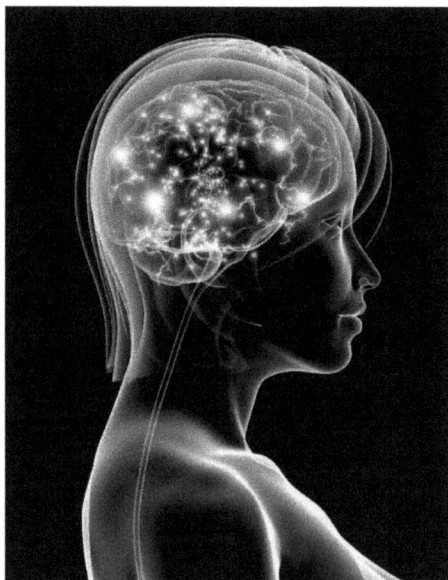

---

[87] http://www.zenlama.com/the-beginners-guide-to-binaural-beats-brainwave-entrainment/
[88] http://www.themorrymethod.com/
[89] http://www.mindpowermp3.com/What-is-brainwave-entrainment.html

Harmonics

Jonathan Goldman is an author, musician and teacher in the fields of Harmonics and Sound Healing.

In 2011, he was listed by the Watkins Review as one of the 100 most spiritually influential people in the world. [90]

Completing a Masters Degree program (an Independent Study from Lesley University) researching the Uses of Sound and Music for Healing, he founded the Sound Healers Association in 1982. [91]

He also began recording his own music under his own record label (Spirit Music); one of the first record labels dedicated to the therapeutic use of sound and music. [92]

---

[90] http://en.wikipedia.org/wiki/Jonathan_Goldman
[91] Ibid.
[92] Ibid.

Goldman has a three-part theory that runs beneath all of his written and musical works; [93]

[1] Everything in the universe is in a state of vibration. Everything is in motion and produces a sound or frequency. This includes the various parts of our body, organs, bones, tissue, etc.

[2] When we are in a state of "sound" health, everything in our bodies is vibrating in resonance or harmony with itself. When something is vibrating out of harmony, we call this "disease."

[3] Sound is an energy that can entrain, or change, the vibrational rate of objects; therefore, if something is vibrating out of tune or harmony, it is possible to create the correct, natural "resonant" frequency of the out of tune object, project it to that out of tune portion and cause it to vibrate back to its normal, healthy state. This, in turn, can be summarized as: Frequency + Intent = Healing.

---

[93] http://en.wikipedia.org/wiki/Jonathan_Goldman

Healing Sounds [94]

Healing Sounds Show with Jonathan Goldman [95]

Jay Weidner's Smoke and Mirrors Radio Hour with Jonathan Goldman [96]

Jonathan Goldman's Healing Sounds [97]

Sound Healer's Association [98]

Temple of Sacred Sound [99]

---

[94] http://vimeo.com/39462044
[95] http://www.healthylife.net/RadioShow/archiveJG.htm
[96] http://www.sacredmysteries.com/public/department58.cfm
[97] http://www.healingsounds.com/
[98] http://www.soundhealersassociation.org/jonathan-goldman-9-elements-of-sound-healing
[99] http://www.templeofsacredsound.org/

Hypnosis

Hypnosis, a merged state of relaxation and concentration with a state of heightened awareness, can only be induced by suggestion.

Hypnosis has been in use for thousands of years.

As far back as 1550 BC, Egyptians had sleep temples in which people were asked to lie down and listen to somebody chanting to help cure illness and problems.

The Ebers Papers are one of the oldest human writings dating back to 300 BC; herein, hypnosis is described as a treatment of human illness.

In addition, there is a great deal of evidence to support the belief that hypnosis was being used by the Ancient Greeks and Romans, for therapeutic benefit, as far back as about the 4th century BC.

While your subconscious has the power and knowledge of the universe, it has no imagination, no direction of its own; having plotted your course, it will follow your every command.

The universe is in perfect balance, made up of what we have termed "positive" and "negative" vibrations.

If you seek (or accept) the negative vibrations, this is what your subconscious projects; in keeping, this is what you, in turn, will receive.

Throughout our lives, especially when we are young, we pick up beliefs, both consciously and unconsciously, from society, our parents, our family, our friends and even our own personal perceptions and reactions.

More than any other force, they shape our perception; so much so, that we often are unable to perceive them.

It is possible, however, to change them; in doing so, we can completely alter our reality (and our potential) through the re-programming of our subconscious mind.

Essentially, anything you can do now, you can do better with hypnosis.

———————————�֍———————————

According to Dr. David Spiegel (Associate Chair of Psychiatry, Stanford University School of Medicine) "hypnosis is not mind control. It is a naturally occurring state of concentration. It is actually a means of enhancing your control over both your mind and your body." [100]

———————————✖———————————

The theory behind hypnosis, according to well-known clinical hypnotherapist Wendi Friesen, is that hypnosis can "gently release blocks and fears, and create a new inner belief that will set the wheels in motion to make changes in the way you think, feel and behave." [101]

———————————✖———————————

[100] http://www.ask-the-hypnotist.com/hypnosis-whats-it-good-for.html

[101] http://www.sheknows.com/health-and-wellness/articles/810449/is-hypnosis-good-for-health

Hypnosis, then, is a tool that allows the mind to focus; unlike the popular myths, you are not unconscious while in a hypnotic state, but fully awake and in a heightened state of concentration.

Hypnosis is a way to access your subconscious mind directly to help you reframe the way you think, and feel, about things, replacing negativity with thoughts and feelings that are more advantageous.

⸻ ❈ ⸻

About Hypnotherapy [102]

Benefits of Hypnosis Therapy [103 104 105 106 107 108]

---

[102] http://www.carolinecarr.com/hypnotherapy
[103] http://www.holistic-mindbody-healing.com/benefits-of-hypnosis.html
[104] http://www.essortment.com/benefits-hypnosis-16667.html
[105] http://johnweirhypnosis.com/index.php/benefits-of-hypnosis
[106] http://www.shiftclinicalhypnotherapy.com/5-key-benefits-of-hypnosis/

Benefits of Self Hypnosis [109]

Hypnosis and Hypnotherapy [110]

Hypnosis in the Medical Community [111]

Medical Benefits of Hypnosis [112]

The Top Ten Benefits of Hypnotherapy [113]

---

[107]

http://mindspringhypnotherapy.com/Benefits_of_Hypnosis.html

[108] http://hypnosisjustworks.com/benefits-of-hypnosis

[109] http://www.hyptalk.com/blog/the-benefits-of-self-hypnosis/

[110] http://www.bsch.org.uk/hypnotherapy.htm

[111] https://www.positivechanges.com/hypnosis-medical.php

[112]

http://mooreinspire.com/medical_benefits_of_hypnosis.html

[113] http://connecthypnotherapy.com/10-benefits-of-hypnotherapy

Meditation

The word *meditation* carries different meanings in different contexts.

Meditation has been practiced, since antiquity, as a component of numerous religious traditions and beliefs.

Meditation often involves an internal effort to self-regulate the mind in some way.

Meditation is often used to clear the mind and ease many health issues (such as high blood pressure, depression and anxiety).

Meditation can be a seated practice; so, too, can it be done in an active way (awareness of one's day-to-day activities), a form of mindfulness meditation.

5 Guided Meditations [114]

5 Minute Morning Meditation [115]

7 Health Benefits of Meditation [116]

Benefits of Meditation [117] [118] [119] [120] [121]

Harvard Yoga Scientists Find Proof of Meditation Benefit [122]

---

[114] http://www.ultimatemeditationkit.com/

[115] http://www.the-guided-meditation-site.com/5-minute-morning-meditation.html

[116] http://foodmatters.tv/articles-1/7-health-benefits-of-meditation

[117] http://www.artofliving.org/benefits-meditation

[118] http://www.emmaseppala.com/10-science-based-reasons-start-meditating-today-infographic/#.Uv02F-SYZ9A

[119] http://www.psychologytoday.com/articles/200304/the-benefits-meditation

[120] http://www.project-meditation.org/bom/health_benefits_of_meditation.html

[121] https://www.meditationoasis.com/about/benefits-of-meditation/

[122] http://www.bloomberg.com/news/2013-11-22/harvard-yoga-scientists-find-proof-of-meditation-benefit.html

Mindfulness Meditation Benefits [123]

Mind Games: 7 Reasons You Should Meditate [124]

Research on Meditation [125]

The Guided Meditation Site [126]

What Happens to the Brain When You Meditate (And How it Benefits You) [127]

---

[123] http://www.huffingtonpost.com/2013/04/08/mindfulness-meditation-benefits-health_n_3016045.html

[124] http://www.livescience.com/20920-mindfulness-meditation-health-benefits.html

[125] http://en.wikipedia.org/wiki/Research_on_meditation

[126] http://www.the-guided-meditation-site.com/

[127] http://lifehacker.com/what-happens-to-the-brain-when-you-meditate-and-how-it-1202533314

Mind Movies

When it comes to visualization, yet another medium, I find it incredibly difficult to see the pictures while also trying to put myself in the image.

It is quite difficult to get emotionally excited about a specific impression when all my mind sees are some dark and fuzzy attempts at a new reality.

Mind Movies allows you to transform a boring vision board into a fun, digital video vision board, one that is filled with positive affirmations, inspiring images and motivating music.

Having discovered **MIND MOVIES**, [128] an absolutely phenomenal metaphysical tool, I am finally able to visualize with increasing clarity.

---

[128] http://www.mindmovies.com/?10107

Visualization is the process of using your thoughts and emotions to imagine, and then attract, the people, circumstances, situations and opportunities, you most desire into your life.

Napoleon Hill has been talking about visualization for nearly a hundred years; so, too, has it been regularly used, for decades, by people from all walks of life, to achieve their goals in a much faster, and easier, way.

The secret to effective visualization is two-fold.

[1] You must first create a clear mental picture of what you want.

[2] You must then see yourself having already achieved these results, using deep feeling and strong emotion.

However, being able to successfully visualize your goals in your mind, with complete emotion, can feel impossible for some people.

Mind Movies is a multi-media tool that allows you to create a vision of what you want, scored with your favorite song; the one that makes you feel good, the one that makes you want to dance, the one that makes you smile and sing along.

This is an incredibly fun way to visualize.

Feel free to watch TIME TO REVOLUTIONIZE [129] as well as AN ABUNDANCE OF BLESSINGS, [130] the two Mind Movies that I was inspired to create.

MIND MOVIES MATRIX PROGRAM [131] is an outstanding merger of the original Mind Movies program with the best subconscious programming technology (courtesy of my friend, Morry Zelcovitch) that exists, all to bring you the *ultimate experience* in mentally transforming yourself for success.

---

[129] http://www.youtube.com/watch?v=UBLFLF4c7cU
[130] http://www.youtube.com/watch?v=rHpH3jBBEBY
[131] http://www.mindmoviesmatrix.com/?10107

A Brainwave Entrainment expert, Morry worked with the Brazilian Government to train officers to reach their peak performance. [132]

In this transformational program, you get ……

[1] 4 brand new pre-made Matrix Mind Movies (money, weight loss, relationships, the perfect partner) laced with Brainwave Entrainment programming to physically rebalance your brain so that all of the positive messages on the Mind Movies are absorbed, like a sponge, into your consciousness; your mind, then, becomes conditioned to see opportunities for success in every moment of your life.

[2] 4 pre-made Subliminal Success Mind Movies (money, weight loss, relationships, the perfect partner) whereby Morry has installed subliminal technology into the Mind Movies so that you receive positive audio programming that will bypass any conscious resistance in order to be absorbed by your subconscious mind.

---

[132] http://www.themorrymethod.com/TMMResearch-FIN.3.pdf

This has been accomplished by turning up the audio messages to a higher frequency and increasing the speed to a point where the conscious mind is unable to recognize them, unlike your subconscious mind.

As a result, you are, literally speaking, absorbing over one million messages per Mind Movie viewing.

[3] 4 Subliminal Success audios (money, weight loss, relationships, the perfect partner) that can be listened to while you are also focusing on other things.

[4] Sleep Meditation audio

During your immersion into this success conditioning program, your mind is going to need some help integrating all of the information while you sleep; as a result, Morry created this Brainwave Entrainment audio (one that allows all of the images and subliminal messages to weave themselves into the deepest parts of your mind) that you can listen to right before going to bed.

A program that was two years in the making, all I can say is that this newest version has, by far, totally exceeded *all* of my expectations.

NeuroSensory Algorithms

The quality of your life is directly related to the quality of your thoughts and the fitness of your brain.

Many people spend thousands of dollars to enhance their bodies, yet do nothing to optimize their brain's potential.

Interestingly enough, it has been stated that we can achieve far more in our lives by managing our brainwave activity and developing healthy thought patterns.

NSA technology features deep carrier frequencies. These are the actual sine waves that transport your mind into the deepest meditative states, magnifying the effect of the binaural beats and isochronic tones, thereby allowing you to achieve maximum results in the least amount of time (which means, quite simply, optimum benefit for your brain and you).

NeuroSensory Algorithms can [1] enhance sleep, [2] slow aging, [3] arrest insomnia, [4] reduce stress, [5] boost energy, [6] eliminate jet lag, [7] improve physical performance, [8] enhance memory, focus and concentration, [9] relax and rejuvenate and [10] stimulate creativity.

Journey Of The Soul (one of my favorite programs) [133]

Q Dreams [134]

---

[133] http://infiniteevolutioncenter.com/jos/
[134] http://qdreams.com/

Paraliminals

Paraliminals [135] [136] [137] are CDs that have been crafted using state-of-the-art digital recording equipment to produce a soothing 3-D sound that allows music, voices, and nature sounds to project spatially into your mind.

There are no subliminal messages in Paraliminals.

With repeated listenings, Paraliminals condition us to believe that we will succeed; having that belief is the ultimate conduit to great success.

When you listen to a Paraliminal session, you hear two distinct voices: one in each ear. To get the desired effect of these relaxing, meditative programs, you have to listen with stereo headphones.

---

[135] http://www.stevepavlina.com/paraliminals/
[136]
http://www.learningstrategies.com/paraliminal/article1.asp
[137] http://www.toolsforwellness.com/paraliminal.html

Each ear receives a unique message tailored to a different hemisphere of the brain.

Rather than a series of repetitive affirmations, the messages are intricate and valuable in themselves; they include instruction, advice, and creative visualization exercises.

Many of the Paraliminal CDs include two separate programs (an A program and a B program), thereby providing you with additional variety.

Each CD has a particular theme based on some aspect of personal development (such as overcoming procrastination, improving your memory, breaking addictions, conditioning new habits, improving relationships, attracting financial abundance, and so on).

An effective performance enhancer that can help you draw upon untapped inner resources, a typical Paraliminal session lasts about 20 minutes; some are longer, some shorter.

Subliminals

Subliminal messages are sensory related stimuli aimed below a person's level of conscious perception; the two most common types are visual stimuli (as in movies and videos) and audio stimuli (as in CDs and MP3 audio files).

As far as audio files go, subliminals are affirmations that are hidden inside the audio itself; these messages are hidden in such a way that the conscious mind cannot criticize, or object to, the content, further allowing the messages to easily enter the subconscious in order to change one's thinking and beliefs more readily.

Based on scientific evidence, subliminal messages have an effect when there is an audible track embedded subliminally into the presenting background sound. [138]

---

[138] http://www.mindfithypnosis.com/do-subliminal-messages-work

Triliminals

Triliminals (a form of sound used for reprogramming your mind through the use of affirmations) work on both a subconscious level as well as a conscious level to help unify your mind in its decision making process.

In this way, triliminals are able to bring greater clarity to your thought processes and more decisiveness to your life.

Originally hypothesized by my good friend, Morry Zelcovitch, triliminals work by giving different affirmations, with the same purpose, to both hemispheres of the brain in tandem with the center (non-hemispheric specific) brain; as a result, both your conscious mind and your subconscious mind begin working together. [139]

---

[139] http://quantumtriliminalsuccess.com/Teleseminar2.htm

Each side of the brain thinks differently and usually we give more power to one side than the other.

It has been scientifically proven that those who use both sides of their brain together are often more successful and confident; so, too, are they in control of their lives.

This is the *only* method known to actually involve both hemispheres of the brain at the same time; most methods either focus on one, or the other, to get results. Truth be told, this is why triliminal mind programming is so effective.

Courtesy of independent studies research, triliminals have been scientifically proven to be effective.

By way of further comparison ......

[1] Triliminals are used to *instruct your conscious mind* about what to do; hence, they use the YOU form of language.

[2] Subliminals work on a *subconscious level* of judgment and are silent in comparison (can only be heard by your subconscious brain); hence, they need to use the I form of language.

[3] Quantum Triliminals use three types of affirmations simultaneously, with the intention of *reprogramming the mind.*

Similar to performing a defragmentation on the hard drive of your computer, most quantum triliminal affirmations are thought to work by reorganizing how we store information in the mind.

When we hear the different affirmations at the same time, our mind must work at a higher level to try and comprehend everything; the end result, being that the message is heard by both the conscious *and* the subconscious.

While you need only listen to triliminals on a sporadic basis (meaning two to three times a week), their effects will begin to decrease if you stop using them; similar to exercising your muscles, your brain is also a powerful muscle.

The only time that there may be cause for concern is if you have specific mental impairments; in this case, it would be advisable to talk with a healthcare provider before working with triliminals.

Message 3

CONCLUSIVENESS OF GOD

All have come here to experience and understand the conclusiveness of God in this physical form. If I take the time to see, to feel, to reflect, to meditate within, I will be able to confirm that God exists everywhere, within all things and within all beings.

In paraphrasing the teachings of Ramtha, I am a melding of God-man (the mind of God expressing in human form) and man-God (physical man expressing the God within).

In essence, then, I am a combined merger of both spiritual and physical that serves to continue the expansion of the Father (Abba, Absolute, Adonai, Allah, All-Glorious, All-Knowing, All-Pervading, All-Powerful, All That Is, All-Wise, Almighty, Alpha and Omega, Consciousness, Divine Creator, Elohim, Formless One, Giver of All Things, Jehovah, Lord of All, Master Craftsman, Omniscient, Source, Timeless One, Yahweh) into forever.

Conclusiveness refers to assurance, meaning that all have come here to experience and understand the *assurance* of God in this physical form.

Conclusiveness refers to certainty, meaning that all have come here to experience and understand the *certainty* of God in this physical form (along with what we create).

Conclusiveness refers to something that convinces, meaning that all have come here to experience and understand the *conclusive evidence* of God in this physical form.

If I come from the Absolute, everything (everyone) is the Absolute; unfortunately, a great many continue to see only from the Veil of the Relative (or separation) in that they see themselves as independent and separate entities.

There is only Consciousness.

There is only the essence of myself expressed as individuated aspects of the same.

There is only the Absolute.

The Absolute is Consciousness manifested in human form.

With each lifetime, we continue to expound (and express) until our final return into the formlessness from whence we came; we are merely players in this game of nonduality.

In the words of Mastin Kipp [140] ... *We at The Daily Love refer to the Universe as the Uni-verse. Why is this? We like to point out the obvious beauty in this simple word. Uni = one. Verse = song. Together, in all our own unique ways, we are all participating in One Song. We believe that underlying and orchestrating this One Song is a creative and benevolent Presence that has our best interest in mind. We use the word Uni-verse to highlight our similarities and as an attempt to reference this Presence without any dogma, stigma or other associations.*

We wish to point out what we lovely and amazing human beings have in common, rather than highlight any differences.

---

[140] http://thedailylove.com/why-uni-verse/

We feel that the word Uni-verse is our little part to help create a new vocabulary that unites instead of divides our many diverse cultures, traditions and faiths.

NONDUALITY

A Society of Souls: The School for Nondual Healing and Awakening [141]

Awakened Clarity Now [142]

Enlightenment Podcast [143]

Esoteric Science: Self-Realization and Nonduality [144]

Francis Lucille [145]

---

[141] http://societyofsouls.com/programs/ikh-training-overview
[142] http://awakeningclaritynow.com/
[143] http://www.enlightenmentpodcast.com/nonduality/
[144] http://www.esotericscience.org/articlei.htm
[145] http://www.francislucille.com/

Gurudatta Dattatreya [146] [147]

Institute of Spiritual Awakening [148]

Jed McKenna`s Theory of Everything [149]

Jeff Foster [150]

Living Nonduality (Robert Wolfe) [151]

Nondual Awareness [152]

Nondual Emptiness Teachings [153]

---

[146] https://www.facebook.com/omgurudatta
[147]

http://www.youtube.com/watch?v=Ed2xlKSFwpY&feature
=c4-overview&list=UU9GKH2WG7i6KhNb8CqQuCrA
[148] http://www.ispiritualawakening.org/
[149] http://www.wisefoolpress.com/toe/
[150] http://www.lifewithoutacentre.com/
[151] http://www.livingnonduality.org/
[152]

http://www.innerfrontier.org/Practices/NonDualAwareness.h
tm
[153] http://www.heartofnow.com/files/emptiness.html

Nonduality [154]

Nonduality America [155]

Nonduality Contemplation and Teachings (Rupert Spira) [156]

Nonduality Highlights (Jerry Katz) [157]

Nonduality In A Nutshell [158]

Nonduality Institute [159]

Nonduality Magazine [160]

Nonduality Network Talk Radio (Jerry Katz) [161]

Nonduality Press [162]

---

[154] http://peliguin.com/nonduality/
[155] http://nondualityamerica.wordpress.com/
[156] http://non-duality.rupertspira.com/home
[157] http://groups.yahoo.com/neo/groups/NDhighlights/info
[158] http://kiloby.com/writings.php?writingid=170
[159] http://nondualityinstitute.org/
[160] http://www.nondualitymagazine.org/
[161] http://nonduality.net/
[162] http://non-dualitypress.org/

Nonduality Satsang Nova Scotia (Jerry Katz) [163]

Nonduality Street (Jerry Katz) [164]

Nonduality Talk (Jerry Katz) YouTube [165]

Nonduality: The Varieties of Expression (Jerry Katz) [166]

Nothing Exists, Despite Appearances [167]

One: The Magazine [168]

One with Life [169]

Paradoxica: Journal of Nondual Psychology [170]

Radiance of Being: A Blog on Nonduality [171]

---

[163] http://www.meetup.com/nondualitysatsang/
[164] http://www.nonduality.com/street.htm
[165] http://www.youtube.com/nondualitytalk
[166] http://www.nonduality.com/
[167] http://nothingexistsdespiteappearances.blogspot.ca/
[168] http://www.onethemagazine.com/
[169] http://www.onewithlife.com/p2/nonduality.html
[170] http://paradoxica.ca/
[171] http://radianceofbeing.blogspot.ca/

Scott Kiloby [172]

Science and Nonduality (SAND) [173] [174] [175]

Stillness Speaks [176]

The Center for Nondual Awareness [177]

The Sons of the Law of One [178]

The Voice of Stillness: Nonduality is the Simple Truth [179]

Undivided: The Online Journal of Nonduality and Psychology [180]

---

[172] http://www.kiloby.com/

[173] http://www.scienceandnonduality.com/

[174]

http://scienceandnonduality.wordpress.com/2013/01/30/atman-is-brahman/

[175] http://www.youtube.com/user/scienceandnonduality

[176] http://www.stillnessspeaks.com/

[177] http://nondualcenter.org/

[178] http://www.thesonsofthelawofone.com/

[179] http://thevoiceofstillness.com/

[180] http://undividedjournal.com/

What is Advaita or Nonduality? [181]

What is Nonduality? [182] [183] [184] [185] [186] [187]

---

[181] http://endless-satsang.com/advaita-nonduality-oneness.htm

[182] http://www.stillnessspeaks.com/nonduality/

[183] http://www.lifewithoutacentre.com/essays-transcripts/what-is-nonduality/

[184] http://nonduality.org/what-is-nonduality/

[185] http://welcometononduality.blogspot.ca/p/what-is-nonduality.html

[186] http://www.lookwithinyou.com/what-is-nonduality/

[187] http://www.anintroductiontoawareness.com/Awareness/What_is_Nonduality.html

Message 4

THE CONSTANT CALLED CHANGE

As I come into my own alignment with truth, I am now discovering that anything that does not serve me, anything that is not in resonance with my Higher Self, simply falls away, gradually fading into obscurity.

The attachments that used to immediately hook me into an emotional, stress-filled, frenzy are lessening considerably, for they no longer serve; it is in this release and letting go that something better *always* comes along. I just have to remember to trust.

I know that the only constant in life is change.

In fact, it was Yeshua ben Yosef, the one we have come to know as Jesus, who tried to tell us that we need not fear change because change allows all to Be (as they are) and to Become (who they truly are).

Whenever my existing paradigm (as pertains to either an environment or a situation) is challenged, change is the result; so, too, can it result in fear (of the unknown).

As soon as I make even the smallest change, I have left my comfort zone.

The irony, herein, is that leaving one's comfort zone behind is the very prospect that scares the greater multitude away from living the life they are meant to be living.

If we take the time to look at our lives as an operating system with software titles, in becomes in knowing that "as the world changes and our operating system evolves, applications that used to work may not work anymore; they [may] need to be updated with new codes in order to function in a changed environment. The events in our lives may not seem as straightforward as a few new features in Photoshop, but the principles stay the same; handling a change to the information we use everyday requires work." [188]

There have been many times whereby the psychological distress (caused by change) made it extremely difficult for me to maintain an optimistic outlook; in truth, it felt like an impossible task.

I cried.

I screamed.

I fumed.

---

[188] http://lifehacker.com/5982622/why-youre-so-afraid-of-change-and-what-you-can-do-about-it

I sulked.

After I stopped fixating on what had been lost, I gradually began to find the new situation possible in the sense that it became more livable, more enjoyable, more true to the person that I am continually striving to Become.

In my experience, fear and stress only dissipate when I calm down and embrace the unknown.

It is far better to leave one's comfort zone, in an effort to forge new possibilities, than to remain burdened within the sanctity of the known.

Living life to the fullest is all about growth and growth is not possible without change.

In the fitting words of Karen Kaiser Clark ... *Life is change. Growth is optional. Choose wisely.*

In the wisdom of Winston Churchill ... *To improve is to change; to be perfect is to change often.*

As David Loker shares ... *By embracing change, you allow into your life the endless possibilities that constantly surround us. With change in your corner, anything is possible, you have but to choose.* [189]

As Henri Bergson so intuitively puts it ... *To exist is to change, to change is to mature, to mature is to go on creating oneself endlessly.*

---

10 Ways to Embrace Change and the Crystals to Make It Happen [190]

Change: The Only Constant Phenomenon [191]

---

[189] http://www.greatlivingnow.com/2012/05/23/embrace-change/
[190] http://omtimes.com/2013/09/10-ways-to-embrace-change-and-the-crystals-to-make-it-happen/
[191] http://band-8-ielts-essays.blogspot.ca/2012/08/change.html

Do Your Goals Embrace Change? [192]

Embrace Change: Embrace Prosperity [193]

Embrace Fear and Choose Change [194]

Embracing Change [195] [196] [197]

Embracing Change Mindfully [198]

Freedom and Happiness: Accepting and Embracing Changes in Life [199]

---

[192] http://www.solospark.com/do-your-goals-embrace-change/

[193] http://www.yogitimes.com/article/embrace-change-acircumlembrace-prosperity/

[194] http://theboldlife.com/2012/10/embrace-fear-and-choose-to-change/

[195] http://www.pwpotential.org/embracing-change

[196] http://www.learnmindpower.com/articles/embracing-change/

[197] http://www.secretsoflife.com/2011/08/embracing-change.html

[198] http://www.awakenedlives.com/embracing-change-mindfully/

[199] http://www.sq-wellness.com/blog/2012/03/freedom-and-happiness/

How to Embrace Change [200]

Maintain a Prior Willingness to Embrace Change in Life [201]

Positive Change [202]

Steps to Embracing Change or Becoming a Change Hugger [203]

The Art of Embracing Change [204]

You Either Embrace Change or It Happens To You [205]

---

[200] http://www.huffingtonpost.ca/mike-robbins/embrace-change_b_867258.html

[201] http://www.heartmath.org/templates/ihm/e-newsletter/publication/2013/fall/embrace-change-in-life.php

[202] http://www.internalinsights.com/positivechange.htm

[203] http://www.deborahshanetoolbox.com/steps-to-embracing-change-or-becoming-a-%E2%80%9Cchange-hugger%E2%80%9D/

[204] http://thinksimplenow.com/clarity/embracing-change/

[205] http://www.rawrsavvy.com/you-either-embrace-change-or-it-happens-to-you/

When Change is Stressful: How to Embrace Change [206]

Message 5

BECOMING NONJUDGMENTAL

One of the most challenging tasks we face is to learn to become nonjudgmental.

As I learn to let things be, disentangling from both emotionally charged situations as well as from the collective intellectual mindset of laws, rules and dogma (which is an extremely difficult thing to do), I am able to experience my own freedom and resolution.

When I am willing to embrace the higher vibration, an internal shift in consciousness takes place, thereby enabling me to Become (who I truly am).

When I try to restrict others by judging them, controlling them or blaming them, this limits my understanding of them.

By direct association, my behavior also serves to limit their understanding of themselves.

Just as I am experiencing my own freedom and resolution, so, too, must I allow others the time and opportunity to experience the same.

———————✕———————

Whenever I judge another (or a situation), I am enveloping them within my own belief system; in this way, I find that I am blinded to the truth about them, forgetting that they, too, are whole and divine.

———————✕———————

ACCEPTANCE

Acceptance Is Key [207]

Acceptance: The First Law of Spirit [208]

---

[207] http://zenteaching.com/acceptance-is-key/
[208] http://www.huffingtonpost.com/judith-johnson/acceptance_b_1589391.html

Eckhart Tolle: Spiritual Practices [209]

Growing Personally and Spiritually Through Acceptance and Surrender [210]

Practice Acceptance of What Is [211]

Soulful Living Winter 2009 Featured Articles [212]

Spiritual Philosophy versus Spiritual Practice: The Path to Conscious Unity [213]

The Deepest Acceptance (Jeff Foster) [214] [215]

---

[209] http://www.theendofseeking.net/PR%20-%20Eckhart%20Tolle%20Spiritual%20Practices.html
[210] http://www.eastern-philosophy-and-meditation.com/acceptance-and-surrender.html
[211] http://spiritualityhealth.com/blog/eve-hogan/shatter-your-illusions-practice-acceptance-what
[212] http://www.soulfulliving.com/winter09features.htm
[213] http://www.energygrid.com/spirit/2008/04ap-consciousunity.html?COLLCC=772422753&
[214] http://www.lifewithoutacentre.com/essays-transcripts/deepestacceptance/
[215] http://www.soundstrue.com/shop/The-Deepest-Acceptance/4111.pd

The Key Spiritual Practices of a Personalized and Authentic Evolution Spirituality Lifestyle [216]

The Power of Acceptance: Stop Resisting and Find the Lesson [217]

The Power of Having a Daily Spiritual Practice [218]

BECOMING NONJUDGMENTAL

4 Benefits of Being Non-Judgmental [219]

8 Reasons to Stop Being Judgmental [220]

---

[216] http://universespirit.org/find-out-the-key-spiritual-practices-needed-to-build-a-balanced-integral-and-effective-spiritualized-lifestyle

[217] http://tinybuddha.com/blog/the-power-of-acceptance-stop-resisting-and-find-the-lesson/

[218] http://thedailylove.com/the-power-of-having-a-daily-spiritual-practice/

[219] http://operationmeditation.com/discover/4-benefits-of-being-non-judgmental/

[220] http://www.1millionacts.com.au/inspiration/how-to-stop-being-judgmental

Are You Being Judgmental Without Realizing, Part 1 [221]

Are You Being Judgmental Without Realizing, Part 2 [222]

Are You Being Judgmental Without Realizing, Part 3 [223]

Are You Being Judgmental Without Realizing, Part 4 [224]

A Simple Method to Avoid Being Judgmental [225]

Becoming Non-Judgmental [226]

Developing a Non-judgmental Attitude [227]

How to Be Non-judgmental of Yourself and Others [228]

-----

[221] http://joshuaspodek.com/judgmental-realizing

[222] http://joshuaspodek.com/judgmental-realizing-part-ii

[223] http://joshuaspodek.com/judgmental-realizing-part-iii

[224] http://joshuaspodek.com/judgmental-realizing-part-iv

[225] http://zenhabits.net/a-simple-method-to-avoid-being-judgmental-yes-that-means-you/

[226] http://www.choprafoundation.org/ask-deepak/becoming-non-judgmental/

[227] http://www.wildmind.org/applied/daily-life/mindfulness-and-acceptance

[228] http://positiveprovocations.com/2012/01/15/how-to-be-non-judgmental-of-yourself-and-others/

How To Stop Being So Judgmental [229]

Nonjudgmental Stance [230]

Practicing Nonjudgment [231]

Stop Being Judgmental: Start Being Compassionate [232]

Turning the Stream of Compassion Within [233]

Why Judging People Makes Us Unhappy [234]

---

[229] http://joshuaspodek.com/stop-judgmental
[230] http://www.dbtselfhelp.com/html/non-judgmental_stance.html
[231]
http://www.adeliberatelife.com/live_deliberately/practicing-non-judgment/
[232] http://meghantelpner.com/blog/how-to-stop-being-judgmental/
[233]
http://www.berkeleybuddhistpriory.org/pages/articles/online_articles/oa_turning.html
[234] http://tinybuddha.com/blog/why-judging-people-makes-us-unhappy/

Message 6

REMEMBERING OUR DIVINITY

Many of us have forgotten our divinity.

In so doing, we believe ourselves to be separate from God. Within this forgetting lies limited beliefs, opinions and judgments, none of which are functional in navigating our way through to the higher expression of the God within.

There is a way to remembering the sacredness of all life, and that is the way of nonjudgment.

———————————◆✕◆———————————

As I become aware of my limiting beliefs, I am able to better understand that my interactions with others are driven by what I believe to be true about the person.

Sadly, these limiting beliefs never reflect the actual truth, a truth that states all is one.

As I gain in universal awareness, I quickly come to the realization that my divinity is also theirs as well.

When I respond to people with love and compassion, I readily move from conflict to harmony; such is the very freedom sought by all.

When I remember, embrace and share my divinity, I free others to walk their truth.

I become accepting of their truth, for such is whom they are.

———————— ❯❮ ————————

Awareness Beyond Consciousness: Living Our Potential [235]

Believe in Your Divinity [236]

Deus Nexus: Messages for An Entangled Universe [237]

_____

[235] http://abcacim.org/blog/
[236] http://www.healyourlife.com/author-stuart-wilde/2009/12/lifeshelp/intuitive-guidance/believe-in-your-divinity
[237] http://deusnexus.wordpress.com/

Divine Light Beings [238]

How the Aeons and Other Divine Beings are Sustaining Today's Spiritual Ascension [239]

James Twyman: Peace Troubadour [240]

Multidimensional Humanity [241]

Recognizing Our Divinity [242]

Remembering Our Divine Nature [243]

Remembering Our Divine Self Course [244]

---

[238] http://lightisreal.com/lightbeings.html

[239] http://www.richardccook.com/2013/06/10/how-the-aeons-and-other-divine-beings-are-sustaining-todays-spiritual-ascension/

[240] http://www.jamestwyman.com/

[241] http://blog.peterborysjr.com/tag/divine-awareness/

[242] http://www.spiritualtraveler.com/spiritual_traveler/spiritual_forum/recognizing_our_divinity.asp

[243] http://www.radiorealization.com/

[244] http://abcacim.org/blog/workshops/remembering-our-divine-self/

Remembering Our Divinity [245]

Remembering Our Mission and Our Purpose [246]

Remembering Our Oneness Through Individual Uniqueness [247]

Spiritual Beings Having a Human Experience [248]

The Acceptance Guidebook [249]

---

[245]

http://www.bluestarbornhealer.com/documents/Power%20to%20the%20People!%20Remembering%20our%20Divinity%2011-17-10.pdf

[246] http://yourspiritualtruth.com/2014/01/20/remembering-our-mission-and-our-purpose/

[247]

http://www.keen.com/CommunityServer/UserBlogPosts/Lightwhispers/Remembering-Our-Oneness-Throught-Individual-Uniqueness/605391.aspx

[248] http://emissaries.org/2008/04/27/spiritual-beings-having-a-human-experience/

[249]

http://books.google.ca/books?id=1UGfAdUpTqgC&pg=PA40&lpg=PA40&dq=remembering+our+divinity&source=bl&ots=KV1THg_Qcc&sig=JYEfppExnGAsw0z0pGF5_f1Diqs&hl=en&sa=X&ei=KkLgUuGkOtC1sASbnYGwAg&ved

The Divine Reminder-er [250]

Theosis: Partaking of the Divine Nature [251]

You Are All Perfect Divine Beings Who Are Asleep [252]

Your Divine Inheritance [253]

Your Soul's Plan [254]

=0CFYQ6AEwCDgK#v=onepage&q=remembering%20our%20divinity&f=false

[250] http://divineremembering.wordpress.com/

[251] http://www.antiochian.org/content/theosis-partaking-divine-nature

[252] http://johnsmallman2.wordpress.com/2011/11/13/you-are-all-perfect-divine-beings-who-are-asleep/

[253] http://www.yourdivineinheritance.com/

[254] http://www.yoursoulsplan.com/

Message 7

WE ARE CONTINUALLY EVOLVING

I need to remember that I am continually evolving and changing as per my own individual experience(s).

This also adds to both the greater collective experience as well as the totality of God, which means, as well, that God is also continually evolving and changing.

How could it be otherwise for this loving energy that is ongoing and forever?

Living a life of gratitude, trust, love and peace is what generates more of the same, thereby continuously affecting those around us in a positive way.

Radiating the complete and total realization of being one with the Creator is what enables, and allows, others to feel safe and secure within our presence.

It is impossible not to experience the effects of such love and acceptance.

Long have we been taught to believe that God is perfect.

I believe that a completely different perspective exists; one that many may not be ready for.

God is not perfect, for perfection is naught but a limitation.

If God *were* perfect, there would be no need for God to express through us for the experience.

God simply is.

That having been said, God exists in us, living both through us and as us; hence, we, too, are Gods.

A Major Turning Point in Humanity's Spiritual Evolution Has Been Reached [255]

A Spiritual Evolution [256]

Books by Pierre Teilhard de Chardin [257]

Divine Cosmos (free books) [258]

Principles of Spiritual Evolution, Part 1 [259]

Principles of Spiritual Evolution, Part 2 [260]

---

[255] http://johnsmallman2.wordpress.com/2014/01/08/a-major-turning-point-in-humanitys-spiritual-evolution-has-been-reached/

[256] http://www.spiritualevolution.info/evolution.html

[257] https://archive.org/search.php?query=creator%3A%22Pierre+Teilhard+de+Chardin%22

[258] https://www.divinecosmos.com/start-here/books-free-online

[259] http://montalk.net/metaphys/42/principles-of-spiritual-evolution-part-i

[260] http://montalk.net/metaphys/43/principles-of-spiritual-evolution-part-ii

Principles of Spiritual Evolution, Part 3 [261]

Psychological, Conscious and Spiritual Evolution [262] [263]

Qualities of Spiritually Evolved Human Beings [264]

Reincarnation: The 35 Steps to Soul Evolution [265]

Spiritual Evolution [266] [267] [268]

Spiritual Evolution is the Divine Plan for Life [269] [270]

---

[261] http://montalk.net/metaphys/56/principles-of-spiritual-evolution-part-iii

[262] http://realitysandwich.com/181445/conscious_spiritual_evolution/

[263] http://store.innertraditions.com/isbn/978-1-59143-166-4

[264] http://www.premnirmal.com/qtsofspiritualehb.htm

[265] http://personalityspirituality.net/articles/the-michael-teachings/reincarnation-the-35-steps/

[266] http://www.hermes-press.com/new_evolution.htm

[267] http://www.healinglightinstituteofspirituality.com/spiritual%20evolution.html

[268] http://srisomesvara.org/knowledge/spiritual-evolution/

[269] http://goldenageofgaia.com/spiritual-essays/the-divine-plan-for-life/the-divine-plan-for-life-is-spiritual-evolution/

Spiritual Evolution: The Path to a Meaningful Life? [271]

Spiritual Human Evolution [272]

Teilhard de Chardin on the Planetary Mind and Our Spiritual Evolution [273] [274]

The New Is The Most Exciting You Ever Will Encounter Every Moment Of The Now [275]

The Urantia Book on Spiritual Evolution [276]

---

[270] http://goldenageofgaia.com/spiritual-essays/the-divine-plan-for-life/spiritual-evolution-the-divine-plan-for-life-2/

[271] http://www.huffingtonpost.com/drs-ron-and-mary-hulnick/spiritual-psychology_b_856705.html

[272]

http://www.bernieprior.org/Features/Spiritual+Human+Evolution+SHE.html

[273] http://www.onbeing.org/program/teilhard-de-chardins-planetary-mind-and-our-spiritual-evolution/4965

[274] http://www.onbeing.org/program/transcript/4967

[275] http://lucas2012infos.wordpress.com/2014/01/22/lucas-the-new-is-the-most-exciting-you-ever-will-encounter-every-moment-of-the-now-22-january-2014/

[276] http://truthbook.com/urantia/evolution-and-history/spiritual-evolution

Understanding Spiritual Evolution, Part 1 [277]

Understanding Spiritual Evolution, Part 2 [278]

Understanding Spiritual Evolution, Part 3 [279]

Understanding Spiritual Evolution, Part 4 [280]

Understanding Spiritual Evolution, Part 5 [281]

---

[277]

http://aquariusparadigm.com/?s=Understanding+Spiritual+E
volution+Part+1

[278] http://aquariusparadigm.com/2013/10/27/understanding-
spiritual-evolution-part-2/

[279]

http://aquariusparadigm.com/?s=Understanding+Spiritual+E
volution%2C+Part+3

[280]

http://aquariusparadigm.com/?s=Understanding+Spiritual+E
volution+part+4

[281]

http://aquariusparadigm.com/?s=Understanding+Spiritual+E
volution%2C+Part+5+

The future is yours

---

[282]

http://aquariusparadigm.com/?s=Understanding+Spiritual+E
volution%2C+Part+6+

[283]

http://aquariusparadigm.com/?s=Understanding+Spiritual+E
volution%2C+Part+7+

[284]

http://aquariusparadigm.com/?s=Understanding+Spiritual+E
volution%2C+Part+8

Message 8

THE POWER OF LOVE

God loves us so grandly that we have been allowed, through choice and free will, to create our vast illusions of perfection and imperfection, good and evil, positive and negative.

What does this mean?

To my way of thinking, it means that God, being the totality of All That Is, is the wrong as well as the right, the vile ugliness as well as the alluring beauty, the unholiness as well as the divinity, the illusion as well as the reality.

There simply can be no greater love than this.

I have been entrusted with the power(s) to create that which will enable me to expand in my knowingness.

God allows me to express as I choose, without judgment.

I determine how, and to what degree, I will progress along my evolutionary path, moving past illusions of limitation to the freedom that lies beyond.

I create the life opportunities of my choice.

I determine, and select, which path(s) to take. It needs to be remembered that the primary tool for this journey is naught but life itself.

In the words of Jimi Hendrix ... *When the power of love overcomes the love of power, the world will know peace.*

In the words of Pierre Teilhard de Chardin ... *Man can harness the winds, the waves and the tides, but when he can harness the power of love, then for the second time in the history of the world, man will have discovered fire.*

In the words of Marcel Vogel ... *Love is the glue of the universe and helps keep matter in form. When I love you, I empower you to bring yourself into a state of wholeness.*

Anita Moorjani on Unconditonal Love [285] [286]

A Return To Love: Reflections on the Principles of a Course in Miracles (Marianne Williamson) [287]

Assorted Thoughts on Love [288]

Breathing in Love [289]

Consciousness as God [290]

EFT Mind and Body: Healing Can Begin By Loving Yourself Unconditionally [291]

---

[285] http://www.greatnewstory.com/anita-moorjani-on-unconditional-love/

[286] http://www.mysticmamma.com/incredible-story-of-anita-moorjanis-near-death-experience-and-miracle-healing-from-terminal-cancer/

[287] http://www.peace.ca/a_return_to_love.htm

[288] http://iasos.com/articles/love/

[289] http://www.globalbreathinstitute.com/index.php?page=breathing-in-love

[290] http://www.peterrussell.com/SG/Ch7.php

[291] http://eftmindandbody.com/2012/12/03/healing-can-begin-by-loving-yourself-unconditionally/

Hacking Unconditional Love [292]

I Am The Universe: I Am Love [293] [294]

Love Has No Boundaries [295]

Loving Kindness Meditation [296]

Mettā [297]

Mettā: The Philosophy and Practice of Universal Love [298] [299]

---

[292] http://humanoperatingsystem.org/hacking-unconditional-love/

[293] http://www.cultureunplugged.com/documentary/watch-online/play/50785/I-Am-the-Universe--I-Am-Love

[294] http://www.omniumuniverse.com/Media/Film/

[295] http://zenrevolution.wordpress.com/tag/unconditional-love/

[296] http://www.contemplativemind.org/practices/tree/loving-kindness

[297] http://en.wikipedia.org/wiki/Mett%C4%81

[298] http://www.accesstoinsight.org/lib/authors/buddharakkhita/wheel365.html

[299] http://store.pariyatti.org/Mett257--The-Philosophy-and-Practice-of-Universal-Love--Audiobook-MP3_p_4413.html

Paul Ferrini [300]

Pure Unconditional Love [301]

Pure Love: The Cohesive Power of the Cosmos [302]

Real Power [303]

Spirit Library Messages about Unconditional Love [304]

Spiritual Laws of Love [305]

Spiritual Metaphysics Defined [306]

300

http://www.paulferrini.com/html/body_the_power_of_love.html

[301] http://www.ourultimatereality.com/pure-unconditional-love.html

[302] http://ascension-research.org/love.html

[303] http://godlovesu.com/real_power.htm

[304] http://spiritlibrary.com/tags/unconditional-love

[305] http://www.thehealingpoweroflove.com/spiritual.htm

306

http://www.infinitebeing.com/0612/spiritualmetaphysics.htm

The Entrance to Oneness [307]

The Nature of Unconditional Love [308]

The Practice of Loving Kindness (Mettā) [309]

The Principle of Unconditional Love [310]

The Power of Love (outstanding 3 part series bundle Panache Desai that can be purchased) [311]

The Power of Love Movie [312]

---

[307] http://www.ramdass.org/the-entrance-to-oneness/
[308] http://lightomega.org/Ind/Nature-of-Unconditional-Love.html
[309]

http://www.accesstoinsight.org/lib/authors/nanamoli/wheel007.html
[310]

http://www.spiritualmaturity.info/Unconditional_Love.html
[311] http://www.panachedesai.com/products/detail/the-power-of-love-series-bundle
[312] http://www.thepoweroflovemovie.com/

The School of Love [313]

The Seven Doorways to Love: How to Ignite the Energy of Love Inside [314]

Unconditional Love [315] [316] [317] [318] [319] [320] [321] [322] [323] [324]

---

[313] http://sufism.org/articles/loves-universe-by-kabir-helminski-2

[314] http://life.gaiam.com/article/seven-doorways-love-how-ignite-energy-love-inside

[315] http://www.spellsandmagic.com/Unconditional_Love.html

[316] http://globalpeacemovementnow.com/blog/unconditional-love/

[317] http://www.gatherinsight.com/freshinsights/alison_james/unconditional-love.html

[318] http://www.maximumstrengthpositivethinking.com/Unconditional_love.htm

[319] http://love-and-harmony.org/tag/unconditional-love/

[320] http://www.ascensionlovespirituality.com/Love/unconditionallove.htm

[321] http://www.shiftfrequency.com/tag/unconditional-love/

[322] http://www.nyspirit.com/issue/167/vibrational-healing/unconditional-love

Unconditional Love and Forgiveness [325]

Unconditional Love: The Law of Attraction and You, Part 1 [326]

Unconditional Love: The Law of Attraction and You, Part 2 [327]

Universal Unconditional Love [328]

What Is Real Love? [329] [330]

What Is Unconditional Love? [331]

---

[323] http://www.souls-r-we.net/UnconditionalLove.html

[324] http://manuel.sekmeth.com/inspire/love.htm

[325] http://freedominlight.webs.com/universallight.htm

[326] http://www.abundance-and-happiness.com/unconditional-love.html

[327] http://www.abundance-and-happiness.com/unconditional-love-2.html

[328] http://anotherwaytolive.net/axPostDetails.php?pageId=13

[329] http://www.reallove.com/about.asp

[330] http://www.reallove.com/default.asp

[331] http://www.conversationswithuniverse.com/messages-from-the-universe/bits-unconditional-love/

Message 9

THE POWER OF THOUGHT

THOUGHTS ARE POWERFUL, THOUGHTS ARE TANGIBLE, THOUGHTS ARE THINGS.

Aside from love, on an immaculately grand scale, thought also holds all matter together, for this, too, is what God is.

It is known that thought must first exist before manifestation of thought, also known as creation, can take place. In that alignment, I have the ability to manifest whatever I wish, all for the sole purpose of enhancing the wisdom that I continue to accrue, life after life after life.

I create my life through my thought processes.

Everything I think, I will feel.

Everything I feel, I will manifest.

Everything I manifest serves to create the condition(s) of my life.

———————— ⋇ ————————

Every word I utter expresses some feeling within my soul.

Every word I utter serves to create the conditions of my life.

This is a direct fusion of thought with emotion.

———————— ⋇ ————————

Many will have heard the phrase *like attracts like*, which means that what one gives thought to attracts, unto itself, the very same.

In the end, what I attract into my life is still a matter of choice and free will.

———————— ⋇ ————————

Thought is the true giver of life that never dies, that can never be destroyed; all have used it to think themselves into life, for thought is your link to the mind of God.

We get what we speak.

We are what we think.

We become what we direct our energies to.

We become that which we conclude ourselves to be.

That having been said, I AM THAT I AM is not a phrase to be taken lightly.

Hence, we are neither slave, nor servant.

By comparison, we are sovereign and masterful beings.

We are the creators and directors of our lives. We write the script and decide who plays the roles assigned to them.

If we *truly realized* how powerful (real, tangible) our thoughts were, those thoughts would change drastically.

Perhaps we need to give careful consideration to choosing our thoughts (words, actions) wisely.

In the words of Bob Proctor ... *Thoughts become things. If you see it in your mind, you will hold it in your hand.*

In the words of James Allen ... *All that a man achieves and all that he fails to achieve is the direct results of his own thoughts.*

In the words of Zig Ziglar ... *You are what you are and where you are because of what has gone into your mind. You can change what you are and where you are by changing what goes into your mind.*

In the words of Mahatma Gandhi ... *A man is but the product of his thoughts. What he thinks, he becomes.*

In the words of Ralph Waldo Emerson ... *Thought is the blossom; language the bud; action the fruit behind it.*

———————— ❖ ————————

Clearly, we are the architects of our own mind.

Reality, then, appears to consist of both mind and matter, whereby it is the mind that influences matter.

Your mind is your reality; change your mind and so, too, must your reality change.

It is my personal belief that mind and matter are the same thing, but only *from a metaphysical standpoint* as opposed to a physical perspective.

Altering Matter and Energy with Effortlessness [332]

Buddhism, Quantum Physics and Mind [333]

Can Thoughts Make Things Happen? [334]

Consciousness and Quantum Mechanics [335]

---

[332] http://www.mindreality.com/altering-matter-and-energy-with-effortlessness
[333] http://rational-buddhism.blogspot.ca/2012/01/buddhism-quantum-physics-and-mind.html
[334] http://www.finerminds.com/manifesting/law-of-attraction-skeptic/
[335] http://www.integralscience.org/ConsciousQM.html

Consciousness and Reality [336]

Consciousness and The Physical World [337]

Consciousness Technologies and Research [338]

Difference Between Thoughts and Beliefs [339]

Does Mind Create Reality? [340]

How Do Thoughts Become Things? [341] [342]

How the Power of Intention Alters Matter [343]

---

[336] http://www.peterrussell.com/Reality/RHTML/R2.php

[337] http://www.newdualism.org/papers/D.Stokes/ConsciousnessandthePhysicalWorld-book.htm

[338] http://www.psyleron.com/info/research/index.html

[339] http://www.mindreality.com/difference-between-thoughts-and-beliefs

[340] http://www.christiandequincey.com/iQNoeticNews/?p=4179

[341] http://www.metaphysics-for-life.com/thoughts-become-things.html

[342] http://theawareshow.com/2009/04/how-do-thoughts-become-things/

[343] http://www.spiritofmaat.com/archive/mar2/tiller.htm

How Thoughts Become Things [344] [345]

How Your Thoughts Become Things [346]

Inner Vision: The Mind [347]

John Hagelin on The Unified Field [348]

Law of Attraction Quantum Physics Guide for Beginners [349]

Mind and Matter [350] [351]

---

[344] http://www.howthoughtsbecomethings.com/

[345] http://www.whitedovebooks.co.uk/2013/07/law-of-attraction-how-thoughts-become-things/

[346] http://www.nateleung.com/how-your-thoughts-become-things/

[347] http://www.edgarcayce.org/ps2/innervision_mind_J_Van_Auken.html

[348] http://www.goodvibeuniversity.com/public/John_Hagelin_on_the_Unified_Field.cfm

[349] http://www.mindbridge-loa.com/Law-of-Attraction-Quantum-Physics-for-beginners.html

[350] http://www.budsas.org/ebud/whatbudbeliev/73.htm

Mind and Matter, Part 1 [352]

Mind and Matter, Part 2 [353]

Mind Is Matter [354] [355]

Mind Moves Matter [356]

Mind Over Matter [357] [358] [359] [360]

---

[351]

http://www.trans4mind.com/personal_development/Philos/
MindMatter.htm
[352]

http://www.advaita.org.uk/discourses/sadananda/mind_matt
er1_sadananda.htm
[353]

http://www.advaita.org.uk/discourses/sadananda/mind_matt
er2_sadananda.htm
[354] http://thehumanist.org/november-december-2013/mind-
is-matter/
[355] http://www.ramnarayanram.com/mind-is-a-matter.html
[356] http://www.pradeepaggarwal.com/mind-moves-
matter.htm
[357] http://www.youtube.com/watch?v=ZdEl8OlQlLc
[358] http://www.collective-evolution.com/2013/09/05/mind-
over-matter-princeton-russian-scientist-reveal-the-secrets-
of-human-aura-intentions/

Mind Over Matter: How the Human Mind Creates Your Experience of Physical Reality [361]

Possible Bridge Between the Mind and Matter (American Journal of Physical Chemistry) [362]

Power of Thought: A Quantum Perspective [363]

Quantum Physics [364]

---

[359] http://www.motivation-for-dreamers.com/mind-over-matter.html

[360] http://www.affirmations-for-radical-success.com/mind-over-matter.html

[361] http://www.metaphysics-for-life.com/mind-over-matter.html

362

http://article.sciencepublishinggroup.com/pdf/10.11648.j.ajpc.20130205.14.pdf

[363] http://www.youtube.com/watch?v=FeFuc-qFKoA

364

http://www.pbs.org/wgbh/nova/search/results/?x=0&y=0&q=quantum%20physics

Quantum Physics and Buddha: Why Law of Attraction Is A Reality [365]

Quantum Physics: Sensing Unbroken Wholeness [366]

Quantum Physics, Spirituality and Your Life Experience [367]

Quantum Physics Wave Particle Duality Consciousness [368]

Richard Feynman Experiment Recreated [369]

Right Being + Right Thought + Quantum Physics = Success, Guaranteed [370]

365

http://voyagegroupin.wordpress.com/2013/11/19/quantum-physics-and-buddha-why-law-of-attraction-is-a-reality/
366 http://www.expressionsofspirit.com/quantumphysics.htm
367 http://www.abundance-and-happiness.com/quantum-physics.html
368 http://rickzepeda.hubpages.com/hub/Quantum-Physics-Wave-Particle-Duality-Consciousness
369 http://www.huffingtonpost.com/2013/03/17/physicist-richard-feynman-thought-experiment_n_2883913.html
370 http://www.amazinguniversetv.com/wisdom-of-life/metaphysics-quantum-physics/item/301-right-being-right-thought-quantum-physics-success-guaranteed

The Alchemy of Quantum Physics [371]

The Awakening: Quantum Mechanics of the Human Brain and Consciousness [372]

The Power of Thoughts [373]

The Self as Creator [374]

The Universe is Mental: Secrets of Mind and Reality (Enoch Tan) [375]

Thoughts Are Physical Things [376]

---

[371] http://theoracleslibrary.com/2013/12/14/the-alchemy-of-quantum-physics/
[372] http://endgametime.wordpress.com/the-awakening-quantum-mechanics-of-the-human-brain-and-consciousness/
[373] http://theoccultnetwork.com/the-power-of-thoughts-thoughts-become-things-into-reality/
[374]

http://www.roadmaptoreality.com/Observer_Worldview.htm
[375] http://www.mindreality.com/mindreality.pdf
[376] http://www.edeycaldwell.com/thoughts-are-physical-things/

Thoughts Are Things [377] [378]

Thoughts Become Things [379] [380]

Thoughts Become Things, Choose The Good Ones [381]

Thoughts Become Things, So Think Positive [382]

Thoughts Become Things, Think The Good Thoughts [383]

Using Quantum Physics [384]

---

[377] http://thougthsarethings.blogspot.ca/
[378] http://personalgrowthpeople.com/thoughts-are-things-and-their-effect-upon-your-life/
[379] http://www.lawofattraction123.com/thoughts-become-things-2.html
[380] http://spiritualjourneyguide.com/2013/01/09/thoughts-become-things/
[381] http://www.examiner.com/article/thoughts-become-things-choose-the-good-ones
[382] http://www.gotothings.com/motivation/thoughts-become-things.htm
[383] http://salomeponline.com/thought-become-things-think-the-good-thoughts/
[384] http://iempowerself.com/54_quantum_physics.html

What is Quantum Physics? [385]

When Mind Becomes Matter [386]

Why You Should Be Aware of Quantum Physics [387]

When Your Thoughts Become Things [388]

Why the Power of Mind Over Matter is Important [389]

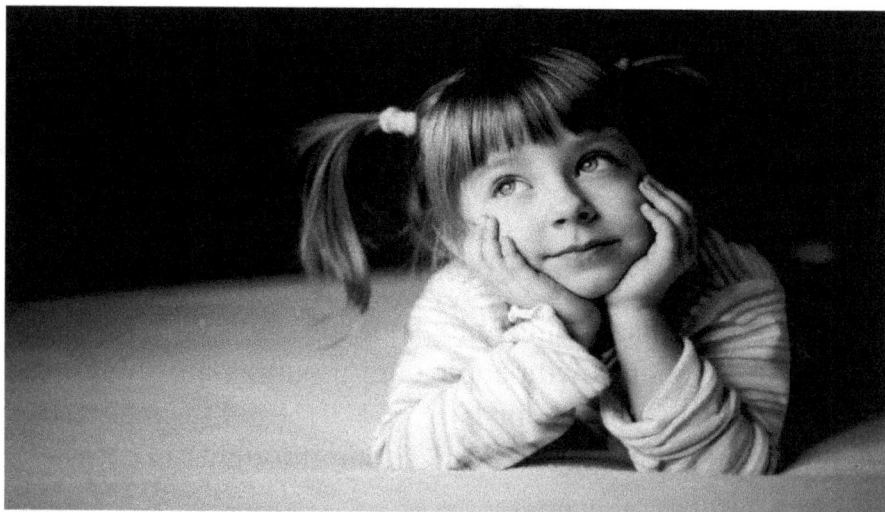

---

[385] http://www.metaphysicalteachers.com/quantun-physics/
[386] http://kabbalahstudent.com/when-mind-becomes-matter/
[387] http://johnassaraf.com/law-of-attraction/why-you-should-be-aware-of-quantum-physics-2
[388] http://www.ecomall.com/greenshopping/gupta2.htm
[389] http://www.activistpost.com/2011/04/why-power-of-mind-over-matter-is.html

Message 10

IT ALL COMES DOWN TO PERSONAL CHOICE

While many continue to accept limiting thoughts into their lives, of which there are a significant number (such as fear, guilt, despair, unworthiness, failure, worry, unhappiness, pity, misery, hatred, dissension and denial of self), it must be remembered that this is neither good nor bad; coming from a place of nonjudgment, it simply is.

In the end, we must remember that everything comes down to personal choice.

Ultimately, I can create a heaven on earth for myself just as easily as I can create my own hell.

The creator of my world(s), I am part of all that I physically see and all that has ever been.

Message 11

GOD IS THE REALITY OF ALL THOUGHTS

Here is another profound truth.

While all things are derived from thought, which is God, it is equally important to realize that God is not simply one formulated thought, but the reality of all thoughts.

Individual truths, as held by you, as held by me, are all true, for each expresses the truth(s) of one's experience at any given moment in time.

While there is truth in all things, so, too, is there refinement in all things. In fact, each moment serves to refine truth, which is why God is not a state of perfection, but rather a state of Becoming.

Message 12

YOU ARE YOUR GREATEST TEACHER

I am here to inevitably learn is that I, alone, am my greatest teacher; so, too, am I my greatest friend.

It is imperative that I cease looking outside of myself, for the path that I am to follow resides within.

Only I can know what is needed for my own soul fulfillment.

———————————✕———————————

It is a feeling, a knowingness; to know your truth is also to feel your truth.

This is why I can say to you: seek that which feels right within your soul.

Believe in yourself.

Be willing to Become unlimited in your truth, remembering, always, that truth is ongoing, evolving, being created every moment by every thought you have.

As an avid reader and researcher, there are many books, many courses, many programs, many subjects and many transformational tools that I have explored over the course of my spiritual journey these past 20+ years; all have served to assist me, to empower me, in the course of re-discovering the truth of who I AM.

You will know what resonates with you.

As a means of further demonstration, it was Leonardo da Vinci who supposedly uttered these fine words … *Realize that everything connects to everything else.*

So, too, for these words belonging to Aristotle … *The high-minded man must care more for the truth than for what people think.*

It was Socrates who spoke of the importance of *knowing thyself*, one of the Delphic maxims [390] inscribed in the pronaos of the Temple of Apollo at Delphi.

In 1831, Ralph Waldo Emerson wrote a poem entitled Γνῶθι Σεαυτόν, or Gnothi Seauton; an anthem to Emerson's belief that to know thyself meant knowing the God which Emerson felt existed within each person.

In the words of Ralph Waldo Emerson ... *Do not go where the path may lead; go instead where there is no path and leave a trail.*

In summation, would you rather be heard or be herd?

To *be yourself* or to *know yourself* ... can one even be separated from the other?

---

[390] http://en.wikipedia.org/wiki/Delphic_maxims

According to Osho ... *Do you think they are different? How can you know yourself if you are not yourself? And vice versa: how can you be yourself if you don't know who you are? To be thyself and to know thyself are not two separate things, hence the question of choice does not arise. They are two aspects of a single process. You have to work on both together simultaneously; neither can be neglected.*

Being In Control of Your Reality at All Times [391]

Be Your Own Guru [392] [393] [394] [395] [396] [397] [398]

---

[391] http://www.mindreality.com/being-in-control-of-your-reality-at-all-times

[392] http://www.dailyom.com/cgi-bin/courses/courseoverview.cgi?cid=257

[393] http://www.awarenessmag.com/janfeb6/jf6_from_heart_love.html

[394] http://www.psychologytoday.com/blog/awake-the-wheel/201007/be-your-own-guru

[395] http://www.erinpavlina.com/blog/2011/01/be-your-own-personal-guru/

Follow Your Heart and Life Will Follow [399]

From Ego to Heart, Part 1 [400]

From Ego to Heart, Part 2 [401]

From Ego to Heart, Part 3 [402]

From Ego to Heart, Part 4 [403]

Journey Into Your Heart [404]

---

[396] http://www.positivityblog.com/index.php/2009/05/20/be-your-own-guru/

[397] http://www.dolivpublishing.com/writersblock/be-your-own-guru/

[398] http://thewellnessproject.net.au/be-your-own-guru/

[399] http://soulhiker.com/2009/08/follow-your-heart-and-life-will-follow/

[400] http://www.jeshua.net/lightworker/jeshua6.htm

[401] http://www.jeshua.net/lightworker/jeshua7.htm

[402] http://www.jeshua.net/lightworker/jeshua8.htm

[403] http://www.jeshua.net/lightworker/jeshua8a.htm

[404]

http://www.livinglifefully.com/flo/flojourneyintoyourheart.htm

Living A Fulfilling Life [405]

Living From The Heart [406] [407]

The Breakthrough Experience: A Revolutionary New Approach to Personal Transformation (John F. Demartini) [408]

The Foundation of Love: Releasing Judgments and Expectations [409]

The Naked Monk [410]

The Only Spiritual Guru You Will Ever Need [411]

---

[405] http://www.lifeoptimizer.org/2008/04/15/living-a-fulfilling-life-a-guide-to-following-your-heart/
[406] http://www.livingfromtheheart.com/Welcome.html
[407] http://www.appliedmeditation.org/LFTH/chap1.htm
[408] http://www.peace.ca/breakthroughexperience.htm
[409] http://tinybuddha.com/blog/the-foundation-of-love-releasing-judgments-and-expectations/
[410] http://www.thenakedmonk.com/
[411] http://www.deliberatereceiving.com/your-best-guru.html#axzz2rMLvZRmz

To Know Thyself [412]

True Heart Meditation [413]

You Are Your Own Guru [414]

You Are Your Own Master [415]

You Are Your Own Spiritual Teacher [416]

You Have To Be Your Own Teacher [417]

Why Being in Your Heart is Better Than in Your Head [418]

---

[412] http://toknowthyself.org/

[413] http://www.spiritlauncher.com/2013/07/true-heart-meditation.html

[414] http://nadineleenutrition.com/3190/you-are-your-own-guru-yes-you-have-all-the-answers/

[415] http://www.buddhanet.net/bvk_study/bvk203.htm

[416] http://noetic.org/discussions/open/164/

[417] http://www.jkrishnamurti.org/krishnamurti-teachings/view-daily-quote/20090713.php?t=Life

[418] http://www.oprah.com/spirit/Listen-to-Your-Heart-Not-Your-Head

Message 13

THE TRUTH PARADOX

While there is a paradox associated with truth, so, too, is it a profound truth, no matter how contradictory the words that follow may appear.

When you have come to understand that *everything is true and yet nothing is true*, you shall be able to see that just as you perceive truth to be whatever you determine it to be, so may all.

In continuation with this explanation, in the moment that you no longer give credence to a truth, it is no longer real, for you have since moved toward a new truth.

When you come to understand that truth is, and can be, all things, then you are free; no longer enslaved to laws, rules, dogma or intellectual understanding.

To learn to Become multi-faceted in your truth means that you are not one truth, but all truths.

Become who and what you truly are by listening to the God within you.

Become who and what you truly are by knowing and accepting that God speaks through feelings, for they will be your guide to truth, directing you onward toward your individual path of enlightenment.

All Truths Are True, All Paths Are Valid [419]

All Truths Are True, Get Over It [420]

Belief in One Truth or Many Truths [421]

---

[419] http://sitsshow.blogspot.ca/2013/11/bashar-all-truths-are-true-all-paths.html
[420] http://preventdisease.com/news/13/101813_All-Truths-Are-True-Get-Over-It.shtml
[421]

http://www.berzinarchives.com/web/en/archives/approachin

On Truth and Reality [422]

Reality of Truths [423]

Relativism and Ethics: What is Truth? [424]

Theosophy and Truth [425]

The Paradox of Truth [426]

The Truths of Life [427]

---

g_buddhism/world_today/belief_one_truth_many_truths.ht
ml

[422] http://www.spaceandmotion.com/Philosophy-
Postmodernism.htm

[423] http://madthinker.blogspot.ca/

[424] http://www.bigissueground.com/philosophy/cauthen-
relativism2.shtml

[425]

http://www.theosophical.ca/adyar_pamphlets/AdyarPamphle
t_No211.pdf

[426] http://www.divyaakummar.com/test/TRUTH_-
_THE_PARADOX_THAT_SETS_US_FREE.php?main_Pa
ge=98&fileID=1843

[427] http://www.thetruthsoflife.com/index2.html

The Unity of Truth and the Plurality of Truths [428]

Truth [429]

Truth is God (Mahatma Gandhi) [430]

Truth of All Truths [431]

---

[428] http://www.as.miami.edu/phi/haack/UNITYTRU.pdf
[429]

http://www.divyaakummar.com/test/TRUTH.php?main_Pag
e=27&fileID=1649

[430] http://www.mkgandhi.org/ebks/truth_is_god.pdf
[431]

http://www.spiritualforums.com/vb/showthread.php?t=3623
5

Message 14

COMPASSION IS WHO WE ARE

Compassion is who we are.

The keys to compassion lie in our ability to embrace all experiences as part of the One, without judgment.

This is the greatest challenge that all must face as they move towards greater states of personal mastery, which is the return to our truest form.

Demonstrating love through compassionate allowing means that you must love others enough to allow the range of their experience.

Compassion is also what we allow ourselves to Become.

Can You Teach Compassion? [432]

Charter for Compassion Makes Surprising Progress [433] [434]

Compassion and Altruism [435]

Compassion and the Individual [436]

Compassion and the Nature of Healing [437]

Compassion: An Increasing Global Movement [438]

---

[432]
http://www.slate.com/articles/health_and_science/new_scien
tist/2013/10/stanford_compassion_and_altruism_research_ja
mes_doty_and_the_dalai_lama.html
[433] http://www.huffingtonpost.com/karen-armstrong/charter-
for-compassion-progress_b_1382844.html
[434] http://charterforcompassion.org/site
[435] http://heroicimagination.org/welcome/psychology-of-
chang/positive-psychology/compassion-and-altruism/
[436] http://www.dalailama.com/messages/compassion
[437]
http://www.omplace.com/articles/Compassion_Nature_of_H
ealing.html
[438] http://www.huffingtonpost.com/elisha-goldstein-
phd/compassion-an-increasing-_b_807518.html

Compassion for All Viewpoints: When the Jain Principle of Anekantavada Meets Practice [439]

Compassion for Ourselves [440]

Compassion Games: Survival of the Kindest [441]

Compassion: Shifting the Balance from Bad to Good Stress [442]

Compassion Training Alters Altruism and Neural Responses to Suffering [443]

Compassion versus Altruism [444]

---

[439] http://www.huffingtonpost.com/jaina/compassion-for-all-viewpo_b_4402155.html

[440] http://www.cygnus-books.co.uk/magazine/2011/08/compassion-for-ourselves/

[441] http://www.huffingtonpost.com/duane-elgin/compassion-games-survival_b_2133146.html

[442] http://www.huffingtonpost.com/project-compassion-stanford/stress-reduction_b_1677439.html

[443] http://brainimaging.waisman.wisc.edu/publications/2013/WengCompassionPsychSci.pdf

[444] http://www.kgrey.com/2011/04/compassion-altruism/

Embracing Our Common Humanity with Self-Compassion [445]

Evolution of Compassion [446]

Excavating the Heart through Buddhist Mindfulness Meditation [447]

Exercises to Increase Self-Compassion [448]

How To Step Into Your Divine Birthright [449]

If We Could All Tap Into This Quality (which We Can), The World Would Be A Better Place [450]

---

[445] http://www.huffingtonpost.com/kristin-neff/self-compassion_b_1889880.html
[446] http://www.huffingtonpost.com/roya-r-rad-ma-psyd/compassion_b_2992902.html
[447] http://www.huffingtonpost.com/noah-levine/awakening-the-heart_b_852429.html
[448] http://www.self-compassion.org/self_compassion_exercise.pdf
[449] http://www.finerminds.com/spirituality/raise-your-vibration/
[450] http://www.huffingtonpost.com/2013/10/29/why-compassion-is-the-nex_n_4170017.html

Loving-Kindness Meditation and Change [451]

Meditation and Compassion: How Do They Fit Together? [452]

Mindfulness in Everyday Life: Compassion and the Art of Having Fun [453]

Self-Compassion as a Characteristic of Spirituality [454]

Study Finds Compassion Can Be Cultivated in the Brain [455] [456] [457]

---

[451] http://www.huffingtonpost.com/kripalu/loving-kindness-meditation_b_3961300.html

[452] http://whatmeditationreallyis.com/index.php/lang-en/home-blog/item/381-meditation-compassion-how-do-they-fit-together.html?tmpl=component&print=1

[453] http://www.huffingtonpost.com/donna-rockwell-psyd/mindfulness-compassion_b_4356626.html

[454] http://www.learningplaceonline.com/spirit/life/compassion.htm

[455] http://www.huffingtonpost.com/2013/05/26/brain-compassion-learned-cultivated_n_3332521.html

Study Suggests Meditation Could Boost Compassion [458]

The Alphabet of Happiness [459]

The Bodhisattva as Compassion Warrior [460]

The Center for Compassion and Altruism [461]

The Conference That Showed That Compassion Can Be Taught [462] [463]

456

http://www.psychologicalscience.org/index.php/news/releas es/compassion-training.html

[457] http://www.psmag.com/blogs/news-blog/compassion-can-be-cultivated-58355/

[458] http://www.huffingtonpost.com/2013/04/02/meditation-compassion-do-good_n_2993793.html

[459] http://academictips.org/blogs/the-alphabet-of-happiness/

[460] http://www.huffingtonpost.com/lewis-richmond/bodhisattva-as-compassion-warrior_b_1641349.html

461

http://compassion.stanford.edu/programs/researchProjects.ht ml

[462] http://www.huffingtonpost.com/christina-patterson/the-conference-that-showe_b_2260272.html

[463] http://compassioninsociety.org/

The Four Ways of Working [464]

The Heart of Compassion [465]

The Medicine of Altruism [466]

The Practice of Self-Compassion [467]

Understanding Altruism [468]

When Empathy Hurts, Compassion Can Heal [469]

When Mindfulness Meets Compassion: Close Encounters in Contemplative Science [470]

---

[464] http://www.unfetteredmind.org/four-ways

[465] http://rahkyt.com/2013/09/20/the-heart-of-compassion/

[466] http://www.dalailama.com/messages/world-peace/the-medicine-of-altruism

[467] http://www.caringtoday.com/reduce-stress/the-practice-of-self-compassion

[468] http://www.psychologytoday.com/basics/altruism

[469] http://www.huffingtonpost.com/2013/09/07/coping-with-distress_n_3836677.html

[470] http://www.huffingtonpost.com/joe-loizzo/mindfulness-research_b_2092829.html

YMD11 Guided Meditation [471]

Message 15

THE WORLD OF POLARITY

It must also be remembered that, as a result of the perceived polarity of darkness and light, we have been gifted with the opportunity to view ourselves from a different perspective, all of which is both necessary and important if we are to truly know, understand and master ourselves in all ways.

Darkness, as well as light, must be embraced, complete and without judgment; both are an essential part of creation.

If you devotedly believe in a single source of All That Is, if you legitimately believe in the conclusiveness and totality of God, then how can you possibly believe that anything of your experience(s) is other than the same source?

———————❖———————

Live your truth; the truth that you feel inside.

Live it.

Manifest it.

There is no need to seek truth; simply allow yourself to Be.

As long as you look outside of yourself, you will never hear the voice that resides within, the giver of all truth and the creator of All That Is.

Each individual is the true creator and controller of his (her) life.

A Different Perspective on the Universal Law of Abundance, the Law of Polarity and Spiritual Wealth [472]

A Higher Vibration of Polarity [473]

---

[472] http://www.energygrid.com/spirit/2007/08ft-abundance.html?COLLCC=3758202868&

[473] http://spiritlibrary.com/uriel-heals/a-higher-vibration-of-polarity

Duality Answered [474]

Duality, Polarization and Separation within the Morphic Field [475]

Embracing Your Dark Side [476]

In Longing For Inner Peace Don't Neglect Its Polar Opposite [477]

Living Within Polarity [478]

Polarities, Complementaries, Dualities of the Universe [479]

---

[474] http://thepolyman.com/2011/07/duality-answered/
[475] http://heaven-on-earth-international.com/articles/morphic/Duality.pdf
[476] http://www.warriorsoflove.com/embracing-your-dark-side.html
[477] http://www.johnglostersmith.com/in-longing-for-inner-peace-dont-neglect-its-polar-opposite/
[478] http://www.spiritofmaat.com/sep11/living_within_polarity.html
[479] http://paulbrunton.org/notebooks/26/3

Polarity [480] [481] [482] [483] [484]

Polarity and Duality [485]

Polarity Light versus Unity Light [486]

Polarity Pathways [487]

The Game [488]

The Law of Polarity [489]

---

[480] http://www.youtube.com/watch?v=_zQieS3NQFM
[481] http://spiritualseeker.net/page/2/
[482] http://www.stevepavlina.com/blog/2007/02/polarity/
[483] http://www.stevepavlina.com/blog/2007/02/polarization/
[484] http://www.stevepavlina.com/blog/2007/03/polarity-and-your-career/
[485] http://www.cosmiclight.com/ofquasars/polarity.html
[486] http://deusnexus.wordpress.com/2013/08/26/polarity-light-vs-unity-light/
[487]
http://www.polaritypathways.com/connect/recorded_dialogue_calls.htm
[488] http://www.michaelteachings.com/game.html
[489]
http://www.adaliaconfidenceandsuccessblog.com/2012/01/22/laws-of-the-universe-law-of-polarity/

The Law of Polarity: Solving Paradoxes In A Dualistic World [490]

The Middle Way [491]

The Polarity Principle [492]

The Seven Hermetic Principles [493] [494]

Transcend Duality and Rise Above Dichotomies [495]

Transcending Polarity [496]

---

[490] http://www.virtualsynapses.com/2010/06/polarity-how-to-solve-paradoxes-in.html#.UubKJeS9x9A
[491] http://www.teosofia.com/midway.html
[492] http://peterspearls.com.au/polarity.htm
[493] http://www.sacred-texts.com/eso/kyb/kyb04.htm
[494] http://www.mind-your-reality.com/seven_universal_laws.html#Part_2
[495] http://ginigrey.com/spiritualtransformers/transcend-duality-and-rise-above-dichotomies/
[496] http://jjesusprocess.blogspot.ca/2011/08/transcending-polarity-stopping-mind.html

---

[497]

http://www.weboflove.org/inspiring_stories_08/081007_tran
scend_polarization_duality
[498] http://www.thetimeoflove.com/answers/transcending-
what-separates-us/
[499]

http://www.thehealersjournal.com/2013/01/31/transcending-
your-internal-polarities/
[500]

http://www.oocities.org/~yukselisorg/new/ascension011.htm
[501] http://www.eckharttolle.com/article/Relationships-True-
Love-and-the-Transcendence-of-Duality
[502]

http://www.universalpolarity.org/Universal_Polarity_Intro.h
tml

What's Your Polarity, Part 1 [503]

What's Your Polarity, Part 2 [504]

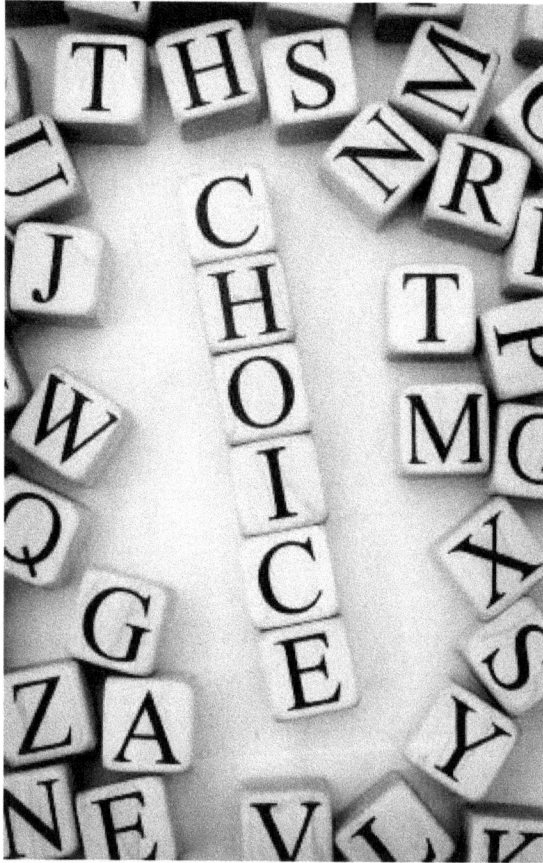

---

[503] http://www.huffingtonpost.com/denise-m-wilbanks/mindfulness-practice_b_4053933.html
[504] http://www.huffingtonpost.com/denise-m-wilbanks/polarity_b_4168402.html

Message 16

THE PURPOSE OF LIFE

The purpose of life is to be part of it.

The key is to live life consciously; likewise, we are to live fully and with intent.

As we continue to expand in both our knowingness and our wisdom, so do we continue to expand the consciousness of all life, which is what God is.

To be happy, to be joyful, to be filled with peace; this is the way back to the kingdom within.

To know that God is not separate from you, to know that you and God are one and the same; this is the way back to the kingdom within.

We are here to live lives of unlimited love.

We are here to live lives of unlimited joy.

If we choose to have these conditions in our lives, then we must first become that which we want to experience more fully.

In summation, then, can it not be said that the purpose of life is to live a life with purpose?

In the words of Aristotle … *Happiness is the meaning and the purpose of life, the whole aim and end of human existence.*

In the words of Eleanor Roosevelt … *The purpose of life is to live it, to taste experience to the utmost, to reach out eagerly and without fear for newer and richer experiences.*

In the words of Maharishi Mahesh Yogi … *The purpose of life is the expansion of happiness.*

11 Actions You Can Take to Discover Your Life's Purpose [505]

15 Questions to Discover Your Personal Mission [506]

Debunking The Whole Life Purpose Thing [507]

Discovering Our Life's Purpose (Jim Self) [508]

Finding Your Purpose [509]

Helping You Find Your Life Purpose [510]

---

[505] http://addicted2success.com/life/11-actions-you-can-take-today-to-discover-your-lifes-purpose/
[506] http://thinksimplenow.com/happiness/life-on-purpose-15-questions-to-discover-your-personal-mission/
[507] http://www.taramohr.com/2013/08/debunking-the-whole-life-purpose-thing-2/
[508] http://goldenageofgaia.com/2010/06/jim-self-on-discovering-our-lifes-purpose/
[509] http://www.radicalmentoring.com/finding-your-purpose/?gclid=CIuJkbG2n7wCFcERMwodn1UAJQ
[510] http://www.psychologytoday.com/blog/prescriptions-life/201311/helping-you-find-your-life-purpose

How to Discover Your Life Purpose [511] [512]

Is Happiness The Purpose of Life? [513]

Life Purpose and Life Intentions [514] [515] [516]

Life Purpose Articles [517]

Life Purpose Books [518]

Life Purpose Calculator (Dan Millman) [519]

Life Purpose Course [520]

---

[511] http://www.stevepavlina.com/blog/2005/01/how-to-discover-your-life-purpose-in-about-20-minutes/
[512] http://www.deliberatereceiving.com/how-to-find-your-life-purpose.html#axzz2rduKuIMs
[513] http://loveofallwisdom.com/blog/2011/02/is-happiness-the-purpose-of-life/
[514] http://www.wanttoknow.info/lifepurposeintentions
[515] http://www.weboflove.org/lifepurposeintentions
[516] http://www.momentoflove.org/lifepurposeintentions
[517] http://www.theonequestion.com/life-purpose-articles/
[518] http://www.theonequestion.com/lifepurposebooks/
[519] http://www.peacefulwarrior.com/life-purpose-calculator
[520] http://www.theonequestion.com/simplepurpose/

Purpose of Life [521] [522] [523] [524]

The Importance of Knowing the Purpose of Life [525]

What Is The Purpose of Life? [526] [527] [528] [529]

What You Need to Live a Life of Purpose [530]

---

[521]

http://www.spiritualresearchfoundation.org/spiritualresearch/spiritualscience/purposeoflife

[522] http://goldenageofgaia.com/spiritual-essays/16244-2/

[523] http://www.share-international.org/archives/religion/rl_swpurpose.htm

[524] http://mettaroundtheworld.org/blog/2014/01/15/the-purpose-and-meaning-of-life-part-one/

[525]

http://www.lifespurpose.info/buddha/sakyamuni/sakyamunibuddha09.html

[526] http://www.budsas.org/ebud/whatbudbeliev/133.htm

[527] http://intentblog.com/deepak-chopra-what-is-the-purpose-of-life/

[528]

http://www.sethlearningcenter.org/q_purpose_of_life.html

[529] http://www.stillnessspeaks.com/ssblog/nityamukta-ananda-the-purpose-of-life/

[530] http://tinybuddha.com/blog/what-you-need-to-live-a-life-of-purpose/

Message 17

WHY ARE WE HERE?

We are here because we wanted to be here.

We are here because we wanted to experience the freedom, and unlimitedness, that God is.

We are here to live.

We are not our successes.

We are not our failures.

We are not our poverty.

We are not our pain.

We are not our joy.

We are not our fear.

These are merely elements of the physical experience that we are here to partake of so that we can know ourselves in all ways.

This is what Yeshua ben Yosef, son of Yosef and Miryam, meant when he said that while we live in this world, we are not of this world.

Meaning of Life [531]

This Is the Buddha's Love [532]

Why Are We Here? [533] [534] [535] [536] [537] [538] [539] [540] [541] [542] [543] [544] [545] [546] [547] [548] [549] [550] [551]

---

[531] http://en.wikipedia.org/wiki/Meaning_of_life

[532] http://www.shambhalasun.com/index.php?option=com_content&task=view&id=2882&Itemid=0

[533] http://www.ted.com/conversations/15635/why_are_we_here_1.html

534

http://www.psychologytoday.com/collections/201112/the-big-question-why-are-we-here

535 http://www.deliberatereceiving.com/meaning-of-life.html#axzz2rduKuIMs

536 http://www.beliefnet.com/Health/Caroline-Myss/Why-Are-We-Here.aspx

537 http://www.exploringlifesmysteries.com/why-are-we-here

538 http://acimexplained.com/the-subject-of-creation-why-are-we-here/

539 http://www.drdavidmutchler.com/?page_id=24

540 http://www.santmat.net/why_are_we_here.php

541 http://spiritlibrary.com/neale-donald-walsch/why-are-we-here

542 http://www.is1.org/whyarewehere.html

543 http://www.oshonews.com/2013/07/why-are-we-here/

544 http://www.spiritualdynamics.net/articles/tag/why-are-we-here/

545 http://bahai-library.com/warwick_meaning_life

546

http://www.innerfrontier.org/Practices/WhyAreWeHere.htm

547 http://www.healyourlife.com/author-dr-darren-r-weissman/2012/06/wisdom/inspiration/why-are-we-here

548 http://www.one-mind-one-energy.com/

549 http://www.sbnr.org/why-are-we-here.html

550 http://www.thevibrantwriter.com/what-is-the-purpose-of-life-why-are-we-here/

551 http://www.spirit-quest.net/2011/01/why-are-we-here-in-earth-school.html

Message 18

THE INDIVIDUAL PATH

The path chosen by each individual is wholly unique to that person.

Each path is a valid one, all leading to the same destination, all leading to one's truest nature, guided by compassion.

This is why it becomes imperative to feel the feelings, to engage the emotions, and to think the thoughts, for they are what allow each of us to experience ourselves in all ways.

The darkness is a most powerful catalyst.

This is something that must be reconciled within each and everyone.

There are many feelings and emotions that find their root in the dark, those that we have come to know as fear, rage, anger, hate, jealousy, depression, control, violation, incest, suspicion, denial, pain, judgment, illness, disease, death, greed, bitterness and retribution.

The darkness is as much a part of us as is the light.

There is, however, a way to avoid the power of this darkness, a power which lies in making choices that do not embrace the dark.

Allowing darkness to exist does not mean that darkness has become your choice.

Allowing darkness to exist does not mean that you have condoned its presence.

Allowing darkness to exist simply indicates that you have acknowledged the reality of this force; a force that actually serves to remind us of the exact opposite.

According to Sal ... *Whatever we deny within ourselves, we see played out on the stage of life as a reflection. That's because our subconscious mind is creating our reality without our awareness. The collective subconscious of all people with terror thoughts will create a reality based on terror. If we do not like the picture we see, we know what to do; change the film (our thoughts). Others may still choose to create terror, but we will be largely unaffected by it if our consciousness does not share it. Eventually, the "hundredth monkey theory" will go into effect and people will suddenly start to realize these truths.* [552]

Sal continues in the same vein of thought ... *Our minds are used to thinking in black and white because we live in a world of duality (light and dark). According to Dr. David Hawkins* [553] *and others, the most enlightened members of*

---

[552]

http://www.salrachele.com/webarticles/theilluminatiandthed arkforces.htm

[553] http://veritaspub.com/

humanity have a greater positive influence per soul than those with a negative vibration have per soul. [554]

Embracing Our Dark Side [555]

Embracing Your Dark Side [556]

Force Power [557]

Force Power: Dark Side of the Force [558]

Force Power: Light Side of The Force [559]

---

[554]

http://www.salrachele.com/webarticles/theilluminatiandthed
arkforces.htm

[555] http://ialarticles.blogspot.ca/2008/02/embracing-our-
dark-side.html

[556] http://www.warriorsoflove.com/embracing-your-dark-
side.html

[557] http://starwars.wikia.com/wiki/Force_power

[558] http://starwars.wikia.com/wiki/Dark_side_of_the_Force

[559] http://starwars.wikia.com/wiki/Light_side_of_the_Force

How I Learned to Love My Dark Side [560]

How to Come Home to Yourself [561]

Integrating Light and Dark [562]

Integrating Your Light and Dark Nature [563]

Light versus Dark [564]

Merlinite: A Stone of Duality [565]

The Dark and the Light [566]

---

[560] http://feedthelovetv.com/2011/07/your-shadow-is-not-your-enemy/
[561] http://tinybuddha.com/blog/how-to-come-home-to-yourself/
[562] http://www.stevepavlina.com/blog/2010/08/integrating-light-and-dark/
[563] http://www.calmdownmind.com/integrating-your-light-and-dark-nature/
[564] http://freedomfightersunite.webs.com/lightvsdark.htm
[565] http://www.healing-crystals-for-you.com/merlinite.html
[566] http://www.divineharmony.org/writings/127-the-dark-and-the-light-v15-127

The Dark Must Be Played Through [567]

The Dark Side of Light [568]

<u>The Dark Side of the Light Chasers</u> [569] [570]

The Key in the Dark: Self and Soul Transformation in the Sufi Tradition [571]

The Spiritual Journey of Darkness and Light [572]

---

[567] http://tucsonshaman.com/articles/darkmustbeplayed.php
[568] http://www.theosophical.org/publications/1375
[569] http://www.thelawofattraction.org/the-dark-side-of-the-light-chasers/
[570] http://store.debbieford.com/product_info.php?products_id=9
[571] http://abwoon.infosaic15.com/pdf/Mainstream/KeyinDark.pdf
[572] http://bobbieslife.wordpress.com/

Message 19

EVENTS IN LIFE SERVE AS CATALYSTS

Every event in life serves as a catalyst that moves us into new experiences of ourselves.

There is no good, no bad, no right, no wrong; it has always been our choice to expand and know ourselves in all ways.

Allowing provides us with the opportunity to transcend the polarities of light and dark, a feat that we accomplish by embracing both as equal expressions of the same force from which we have come.

***

Compassion is our birthright.

Compassion is our truest nature.

Compassion allows us to view from an equal standpoint.

There is no judgment.

All people express their own versions of compassion through the manner in which they conduct themselves in every waking moment.

Are you willing to forgive those who have wronged you?

Are you willing to see beyond hate towards those who have oppressed you?

It is only in answering yes to these questions that you can choose to Become more than the circumstances.

In breaking the cycle of this collective response, one becomes the higher choice.

Mastery of compassion means redefining what your world means to you.

It is not about forcing change upon the world around you.

You, and only you, choose how you respond.

Message 20

WE CAN TRANSCEND THE WORLD OF POLARITY

As a being of compassion, I am offered the opportunity to transcend polarity while still living within the polarity; this is what enables me to move forward with life, a life filled with freedom, resolution and peace.

Compassion means living in trust.

Compassion means living with joy.

Living a new truth must first start with me. I must have the wisdom, and the courage, to embrace this new life, this new truth, as my reality.

This reality must then be lived in a world that may not always support that truth; this was the undertaking of the entire earthly mission of Yeshua ben Yosef.

As shared by Avalon Member PathWalker ... *We are playing a virtual reality game, of duality. In the game of choices, align your choices with your ideals. Everything is whole, complete and perfect; even yourself. Love is the power to change/create.* [573]

As Above, So Below [574]

At the End of the Pendulum's Swing ... Essence Merges with God and all Its Creatures, forming One [575]

Essence of BEing [576]

Polarity: Fourth of the Seven Hermetic Laws [577]

---

[573] http://projectavalon.net/forum4/showthread.php?860-Enlightenment-The-Ego-what-is-it-How-to-transcend-it./page39
[574] http://www.awakened1.net/as_above_-_so_below.html
[575]

http://probablefuture.com/At_the_End_of_The_Pendulum_S wing.htm
[576] http://embracinginspiration.wordpress.com/tag/transcend/
[577] http://spiritofmaat.com/oct08/polarity.html

Polarity Light versus Unity Light [578]

The Adventure of I: A Journey to the Centre of Your Reality
[579] [580]

The Seven Universal Laws Explained [581] [582]

The Spiral and the Holographic Matrix [583]

Transcend Duality and Rise Above Dichotomies [584]

---

[578] http://deusnexus.wordpress.com/2013/08/26/polarity-light-vs-unity-light/

[579] http://www.amazon.com/exec/obidos/ASIN/0957677006/portalsofspirit

[580] http://www.amazon.ca/exec/obidos/ASIN/0957677006/portalsofsp01-20

[581] http://www.mind-your-reality.com/seven_universal_laws.html

[582] http://angellucci.wordpress.com/2013/10/26/the-seven-universal-laws-explained-by-tania-kotsos/

[583] http://www.ascensionnow.co.uk/the-spiral-and-the-holographic-matrix1.html

[584] http://ginigrey.com/spiritualtransformers/transcend-duality-and-rise-above-dichotomies/

Transcending the Hero's Journey [585]

Transcending Your Internal Polarities [586]

---

[585] http://www.themastershift.com/transcending-the-heros-journey/

[586]

http://www.thehealersjournal.com/2013/01/31/transcending-your-internal-polarities/

Message 21

LIFE IS A SPIRITUAL ENDEAVOR

Life is a spiritual endeavor in that I am asked to become that which I most desire in my life.

I am asked to become the peace that I seek.

I am asked to become the compassion that I desire.

I am asked to become the forgiveness that I long for.

I am asked to become the love that is needed.

Be not afraid to demonstrate your Becoming.

The healing of this world will only come about as a result of the healing of thoughts, feelings and emotions.

Who among us is willing to live the truth of a higher response?

Who among us is willing to live the truth of what life has always had to offer?

By virtue of service to self and others, so, too, do we serve the Creator.

In this way, we Become the greatest gift that we can offer.

Our ability to express forgiveness, allowing others the outcome of their own experience(s), without changing the nature of who we truly are, is the highest level of mastery to which all can attain.

Therein lies the healing of all illusion, all separation, all duality.

In the words of Mahatma Gandhi … *You must be the change you wish to see in the world.*

Message 22

YESHUA BEN YOSEF

Yeshua ben Yosef was the eldest son born to Yosef and Miryam.

During the time of his birth, in the year 3 BC, high magnetic values, for the most part, were being experienced across the planet. By comparison, Judaea was experiencing relatively low magnetic values.

At the time of his birth, this was the best possible locale in which to be born, an area where people were *more open and receptive to new ideas*. It is for this reason that he chose to be born in this region.

What is that *you can do* to become more open and receptive to new ideas?

Commissioned by Nick Bunick, author of <u>In God's Truth</u>

Reprinted herein with permission

Message 23

ENLIGHTENMENT

Enlightenment is but a journey of the self.

People everywhere are searching for well-being (meaning, purpose, fulfillment, health and happiness).

For life to be good, we need to feel useful and appreciated.

Taking a spiritual growth journey called *The Soul Journey* [587] will enable you to grasp the bigger picture of who you are, learning how to distinguish your personality from your soul; so, too, will you will learn practical ways to develop and express soul fulfillment for a life of meaning and purpose.

In changing your consciousness, you will have changed your life.

---

[587] http://www.thesouljourney.com/?a_aid=195

In the words of Ralph Waldo Emerson ... *Life is a journey, not a destination.*

The Enlightenment Trilogy by Jed McKenna

[1] Spiritual Enlightenment: The Damnedest Thing [588]

[2] Spiritually Incorrect Enlightenment [589]

[3] Spiritual Warfare [590]

A Journey of Self-Discovery [591]

588

http://www.naturalthinker.net/trl/texts/McKenna,Jed/SpiritualEnlightenment-DamnestThing.pdf

589

http://www.naturalthinker.net/trl/texts/McKenna,Jed/SpirituallyIncorrectEnlightenment.pdf

590

http://www.naturalthinker.net/trl/texts/McKenna,Jed/Jed%20Mckenna%20-%20Spiritual%20Warfare%20HQ.pdf

591

http://www.manifestyourpotential.com/self_discovery/0_start_journey_self_discovery/a_journey_of_self_discovery.htm

A Journey to Self-Discovery [592]

Attain Self Realization [593]

Awakening the Self [594]

Awakening Your Unique Self (online course) [595]

Center of Earth Meditation: A Journey of Self-Discovery [596]

Enlightenment [597] [598] [599]

---

[592] http://www.e-ostadelahi.com/eoe-en/a-journey-to-self-discovery/
[593] http://www.godrealized.com/selfrealization/Attain-Self-Realization.html
[594] http://awakeningtheself.com/
[595] http://awakeningyouruniqueself.com/offer/
[596] http://suzanneliephd.blogspot.ca/2013/11/center-of-earth-meditation-journey-of.html
[597] http://www.pathwaytohappiness.com/enlightenment.htm
[598] http://www.joantollifson.com/writing8.html
[599]
http://www.divyaakummar.com/test/ENLIGHTENMENT_-AWAKENING_-_LIBERATIONION_-_SELF_REALIZATION.php?main_Page=27&fileID=1639

Enlightenment Demystified [600]

Enlightenment Enlighten [601]

Enlightenment Podcast [602]

Going Beyond Illusion [603]

Journal of Enlightenment [604]

Journey to Enlightenment [605] [606]

---

[600] http://www.kiarawindrider.net/planetary-awakening-year-zero/enlightenment-demystified/

[601] http://www.anhglobal.org/en/node/582

[602] http://www.enlightenmentpodcast.com/

[603] http://enlightenmentisreal.wordpress.com/

[604] http://www.selffoundation.com/Journal_of_Enlightment.html

[605] https://www.deepakchopra.com/video/view/545/the_rabbit_hole__journey_to_enlightenment_

[606] http://www.anandaclaritymagazine.com/2012/09/kriyananda-satan-yogananda-joy/

Journey to Kanaka Makua: Rediscovering the Light of Island Wisdom (a game-style method of self-discovery where you can come to higher levels of spirituality and enlightenment as you search to find your own inner truth) [607]

Journey to Self-Realization [608]

Learning and Unlearning: A Journey of Self-Acceptance [609]

Meditations on Ego and Enlightenment [610]

Myths of Enlightenment [611]

---

[607] http://upi.cc/oracle/
[608] http://www.self-realization.in/journey-to-self-realization.html
[609] http://tinybuddha.com/blog/learning-and-unlearning-a-journey-of-self-acceptance/
[610] http://www.globalone.tv/profiles/blogs/meditations-on-ego-and-enlightenment-eric-allen-bell
[611]
http://www.wholebeingawakening.com/Essays/1%20Myths%20of%20Enlightenment/0%20Pretext/0-03%20%20Myths%20TOC.htm

Self-Awareness, Self-Realization and Enlightenment [612]

Self Enlightenment [613]

Self Mastery: A Journey Home to Yourself textbook [614]

Self-Realization [615]

Soulshaping: A Journey of Self-Creation (excerpt) [616]

Spiritual Enlightenment [617]

Spiritual Intuition [618]

---

[612] http://identitywhatisit.blogspot.ca/2011/11/self-awareness-self-realization-and.html
[613] http://www.true-enlightenment.com/self-enlightenment.html
[614] http://www.holisticlearningcenter.com/Self-Mastery-a-Journey-Home-to-Yourself-textbook.html
[615] http://rajeshcmehta.blogspot.ca/2013/01/self-realization-ones-own-journey-from.html
[616] http://soulshaping.com/wp-content/uploads/Grist-for-the-Soul-Mill.pdf
[617] http://stonyhill-nuggets.com/2011/spiritual-awakening/spiritual-enlightenment-the-journey-from-primitive-ego-to-first-awakening-%E2%80%93-part-1/
[618] http://www.spiritual-intuition.com/

The Dream Awakened [619]

The Human Journey: Quest for Self-Transformation [620]

The Journey Beyond Enlightenment [621]

<u>The Journey of Self-Discovery</u> (Bhaktivedanta Swami Prabhupada) [622]

The Path to Enlightenment [623]

The Road to Discovery [624]

---

[619] http://infinitelivingteachings.wordpress.com/
[620] http://www.theosophical.org/online-resources/articles/1702
[621] http://www.nightingale.com/products/journey-beyond-enlightenment/
[622]

http://www.radiokrishna.com/rkc_archive_new/Books/ENG/The_Journey_of_Self_Discovery.pdf
[623] http://www.happy-science.org/the-path-to-enlightenment
[624] http://gnosticwarrior.com/the-road-to-discovery.html

Message 24

AUTHENTIC LIVING

Many of us are struggling because we have forgotten who we are.

As already stated throughout this text, *our true and authentic selves are connected with Source Energy*; this is who we really are.

By comparison, *who we think we are is how we show up in life*; this is how we present ourselves to the public eye.

Who we think we are comes from listening to other people rather than listening to ourselves.

If we are to live in the flow, we must learn to focus on who we are and what we can do in the moment.

***

Authentic living is never about who you are not, what you cannot do, and what you do not have.

When you are living in alignment with Source, you find that you have everything you need.

Authentic living means

[1] acknowledging that life is not always easy (there will be challenges)

[2] acknowledging that one does not always follow a straight and convenient path (one may be asked to live outside the box)

[3] acknowledging that one must allow life to unfold through them (which, along with being the best part, can also be the most difficult)

One's greatness is not dependent on anything that they do, or do not, accomplish.

We are already great; we merely have to live this greatness, by knowing who we are and what we are here to do in each moment; nothing else is required.

Each day brings a new awareness.

In acknowledging this wisdom, so, too, must we come to realize that we are here to live in alignment with who we are.

We are here to live a life of passion, a life of enthusiasm, a life of pure enjoyment.

There is no time for sitting and waiting. Life does not come to us, hand delivered on a silver platter. We must go after what we want in order to live the life of our dreams, the life of our passion.

What is it, then, that makes you feel vibrantly alive?

In the words of Howard Thurman ... *Don't ask what the world needs, ask what makes you come alive and go do that, because what the world needs is people who have come alive.*

In the words of Carl Jung ... *Your vision will become clear only when you look into your heart. Who looks outside, dreams. Who looks inside, awakens.*

In the words of François Auguste René Chateaubriand ... *A master in the art of living draws no sharp distinction between his work and his play; his labor and his leisure; his mind and his body; his education and his recreation. He hardly knows which is which. He simply pursues his vision of excellence through whatever he is doing, and leaves others to determine whether he is working or playing. To himself, he always appears to be doing both.*

---

6 Principles of Authentic Living [625] [626]

9 Ways to Live an Authentic Life [627]

Are You Living Authentically? [628]

Authentic Living [629] [630] [631] [632] [633]

Authentic Living Magazine [634]

---

[625]

http://www.spiralnature.com/spirituality/sixprinciples.html
[626] http://www.robertrabbin.com/description/
[627] http://www.beliefnet.com/Inspiration/Galleries/9-Ways-to-Live-an-Authentic-Life.aspx
[628] http://www.thewellnesswarrior.com.au/2012/12/are-you-living-authentically-3-powerful-questions-to-help-you-find-out/
[629] http://www.voiceamerica.com/show/1304/authentic-living
[630] http://greatday.com/motivate/130427.html
[631]

http://thepersonalbest.com/ThePaths/AuthenticLiving.html
[632] http://www.mindreality.com/authentic-living-choosing-to-follow-your-bliss
[633] http://www.soul-books.com/authenticity.shtml
[634] http://authenticlivingmagazine.com/

Defining Your Authentic Self [635]

Find the Courage to Be You [636]

Live Authentically [637]

Living an Authentic Life [638] [639] [640] [641] [642] [643]

Living Authentically [644]

---

[635] http://www.drphil.com/articles/article/73

[636] http://tinybuddha.com/blog/find-the-courage-to-be-you-4-ways-to-live-authentically/

[637] http://www.alifeonyourterms.com/the-seventh-law/

[638] http://www.rebellesociety.com/2013/07/25/a-self-made-12-step-program-for-living-an-authentic-life/

[639] http://life.gaiam.com/article/5-ways-live-authentic-life

[640] http://www.alive.com/articles/view/21723/living_an_authentic_life

[641] http://www.learnmindpower.com/articles/living-authentic-life/

[642] http://dharmawisdom.org/teachings/articles/living-authentic-life

[643] http://www.positivehealth.com/article/personal-growth/living-an-authentic-life-the-path-to-fulfilment

[644] http://www.livingauthentically.org/all-about-living-authentically/

Seven Great Ideas for Authentic Living [645]

The Art of Authentic Living [646]

Your Authentic Self [647]

Your Purpose Centered Life [648]

What is an Authentic Life? [649]

[645] http://leightremaine.com/seven-great-ideas-authentic-living/
[646] http://alifeofperfectdays.blogspot.ca/2012/01/art-of-authentic-living-how-to-live-and.html
[647] http://www.soulfulliving.com/may03features.htm
[648] http://podcasts.personallifemedia.com/podcasts/214-purpose-centered-life
[649] http://www.huffingtonpost.com/eldon-taylor/what-is-an-authentic-life_b_4346561.html

Message 25

YOU CREATE YOUR REALITY

With every mood that you feel, you are the creator of the resulting experience.

With every thought that passes through your mind, you are the creator of the resulting experience.

In the way you react to any situation that arises, you are the creator of the resulting experience.

All of these circumstances have one single thing in common; namely, how you *react through emotion* is what creates the experience.

———————————❖———————————

Many years ago, when I was still watching the news, I found myself constantly dwelling on the harrowing events and stories from around the world; so much so, in fact, that the news had a negative effect on my life.

It felt as though I was drowning in depression; a depression that affected my sleep patterns, my diet, my exercise, my life.

Unbeknownst to me, this extreme negativity was also serving to create energy blockages that would eventually affect my health.

This is when I stopped buying newspapers and news magazines.

I also stopped watching television and listening to the radio.

By now you know that thoughts and emotions are incredibly powerful.

If we allow ourselves to react negatively to experiences in our lives, dwelling too deeply on those we deem to be gloomy and pessimistic, the energy around us becomes negatively charged.

This only serves to create continued negativity in our lives.

On the other hand, if we can objectively adapt to circumstances and events, without attachment, our experiences will be far richer, and our energy will be more positive for that which we create in our lives.

It is also imperative that we understand that whilst we are generally unable to control the circumstances (family, nationality, religion, country) into which we are born, we still have the power to take the hand we have been dealt, turning it into something far more positive, courtesy of our thoughts, feelings, moods and actions.

Changing our thoughts transforms (changes) our reality.

---

5 Steps to A Quantum Life [650]

---

[650] http://aquantumlife.com/category/creating-your-reality/

Being a Creator of Reality [651]

Conscious Creation [652]

Consciousness and Reality [653]

Create Your Own Reality in 6 Steps [654]

Creating Reality [655]

Creating Your Reality: All You Need Is Your Mind [656]

Don't Confuse Creating Your Own Reality with the Law of Attraction [657]

---

[651] http://www.mindreality.com/being-a-creator-of-reality-position-of-omnipotence

[652] http://www.consciouscreation.com/

[653] http://www.peterrussell.com/Reality/RHTML/R2.php

[654] http://www.pluginid.com/create-your-own-reality/

[655] http://www.halexandria.org/dward003.htm

[656] http://www.huffingtonpost.com/stewart-a-swerdlow/creating-your-realityall-_b_1649933.html

[657] http://www.mortylefkoe.com/dont-confuse-creating/

Do We Really Create Our Own Reality? [658]

How Cutting-Edge Science Proves You Can Create Your Own Reality (introduction to a program called Quantum Jumping) [659]

How Do I Create My Reality? [660]

How You Create Your Own Reality [661]

Philosophy of Reality [662]

---

[658]

http://realitysandwich.com/12915/do_we_really_create_our_own_reality/

[659] http://www.quantumjumping.com/articles/parallel-universe/creating-reality/

[660] http://www.whatismetaphysics.com/law-of-attraction.html

[661]

http://www.newbrainnewworld.com/?Science_of_Conscious ness:Creation_of_Reality

[662]

http://www.commonsensescience.org/philosophy_of_reality.html

Prove To Me That My Thoughts Create My Reality [663]

Seth: You Create Your Own Reality [664] [665] [666] [667]

Science Proves We Create Our Own Reality [668]

The Law of Attraction Library [669]

The Power of Affirmations [670]

The Power of Words [671]

---

[663] http://tkcoleman.com/2011/08/08/prove-to-me-my-thoughts-create-my-reality/

[664] http://sethinstitute.org/

[665] http://www.execonn.com/matt/Docs/SETH99.htm

[666] http://www.sethlearningcenter.org/PLAIN_site/q_create_realityP.html

[667] http://consciouslifenews.com/create-reality-seth/

[668] http://www.deliberateblog.com/2012/10/30/extra-extra-science-proves-we-create-our-own-reality/

[669] http://www.thelawofattraction.org/

[670] http://www.creativepowerofthought.com/2006/12/30/the-power-of-affirmations/

[671] https://www.keen.com/documents/works/articles/spiritual/the-power-of-words.asp

The Science of Your Reality [672]

True Reality Creation, Part 1 [673]

True Reality Creation, Part 2 [674]

You Are The Creator Of Your Reality [675]

You Create Your Reality, Part 1 [676]

You Create Your Reality, Part 2 [677]

You Create Your World [678]

Your Thoughts Do Not Create Your Reality [679]

---

[672] http://www.thespiritualcatalyst.com/articles/the-science-of-your-reality
[673] http://montalk.net/metaphys/68/true-reality-creation-part-i
[674] http://montalk.net/metaphys/69/true-reality-creation-part-ii
[675] http://findingthefield.com/?page_id=136
[676] http://www.eliasforum.org/digests/YCYR.html
[677] http://www.eliasforum.org/digests/YCYR2.html
[678] http://www.wisdomsdoor.com/rc1/hrc1-01.shtml
[679] http://www.elephantjournal.com/2013/07/your-thoughts-do-not-create-your-reality-stupid/

Message 26

A WORK IN PROGRESS

We are a continual work in progress; the choice is always ours.

As Yoda tried to share with Luke Skywalker ... *Try not. Do or do not; there is no try.*

My thoughts + My Action = My Reality (Experience)

Given that one has the power to change their thoughts at any time, so, too, does this change one's outlook (viewpoint, mindset, perception, paradigm) on their reality experience; when you are able to change your thinking (courtesy of your brain), so, too, do you change your life. [680]

---

[680] http://effortlessprosperityprogram.com/wp/ep-forgiveness/

No matter how you may be struggling to turn your current circumstances around, no matter how you may be struggling to improve your lot in life, there *is* a powerful secret that actually changes your brain from a place of confusion, discouragement, or negativity, into a powerful vibrational force that will change your life in ways that you may find hard to imagine right now.

In fact, scientific research actually proves this to be true.

In summation, the formula to a life of prosperity [681] (peace of mind, emotional well-being, happiness, financial freedom) and abundance is far simpler than most people can possibly imagine.

---

[681] http://339150jaf8wnpr27iex9zn3k4e.hop.clickbank.net/

Message 27

YOUR PARADIGM

If we can create the experiences in our lives, so, too, are we the controllers of our own reality (experience).

Everything comes down to belief.

The moment you believe, the moment that you have shifted to an attitude of I can, the moment that you become willing to change (your thoughts, your beliefs, your perspective, your actions, your inactions), taking full responsibility for your life, everything around you begins to change.

The reciting of affirmations, over and over again, serves to implant a new belief; once the deep conviction of *I can* becomes real, your outlook on life, and living, begins to change.

The word paradigm refers to a conceptual framework, a belief system, an overall prospective, through which we see and interpret the world.

As such, one's paradigm determines what they are able to see, how they think and what they do.

For example, how one views the world, by way of a spiritual tradition, is part of the individual paradigm to which they adhere.

Paradigms are relative, subjective and personal.

We assume that the way we see things is the way they really are.

Our paradigms become perceptible to us *only* when we encounter one that differs from our own.

The asking of pertinent questions, such as those that follow, will tell you much about your own paradigm(s).

▶Do you see the world as a battlefield with good forces pitting against evil?

▶Do you see the world as a classroom where you come to learn and are put through a multitude of tests?

▶Do you see the world as a trap, whereby you attempt to disentangle yourself in an attempt to ascend to a higher plane of tranquility?

▶Do you see the world as a partner, attempting to commune more with nature in an effort to become more fully human?

▶Do you see the world as self, an interconnected whole with each playing an important role in the overall script of life?

As well, these are other questions that one must continue to ponder.

▶What do you value?

► What are your needs?

► What are your feelings?

► What matters to you?

► How do you fit into the grand scheme called life?

► How do you know what you know?

► What is truth?

The more you know about who you are, the easier it is to respond (as opposed to react) to life.

Everything we do, and say, is the expression of our beliefs about the world.

Finding and identifying those underlying beliefs leads to both insight and understanding.

As one would expect, paradigms shift when we change from one way of thinking to another way of thinking.

This shift can be compared to a revolution, a transformation, a sort of metamorphosis, if you will.

However, it is not simply something that just happens out of the blue and on its own; instead, it is driven by agents of change.

For the greater multitude, as well we know, change is difficult.

World views emerge to solve problems.

It is not enough to be passionate about the change that is needed, nor is it satisfactory to suppress the voices of those in disagreement.

For an emerging new world view to take hold, the majority have to fully understand (aside from abstract intellect) that the current way of thinking is no longer adequate to solve the problems that they are being faced with.

The Cosmos Of The Soul II

A Philosophical Analysis of Spiritual Awakening [682]

Change The Paradigm [683]

Integral Awakening Home Study Course [684]

Paradigm Shift(s) [685] [686] [687]

Paradigm Shift Central [688]

Paradigm Shift Magazine [689]

Shift the Old Paradigm for Global Awakening [690]

Shifting Paradigms [691]

---

[682] http://thelightningpath.com/stian/open-eyes/
[683] http://1paradigm.org/
[684] http://integralawakening.com/store/home-study-course/
[685] http://theawakeningself.com/paradigm-shift/
[686] http://www.peterrussell.com/Reality/RHTML/R12.php
[687] http://awakeningplanet.com/started-2-2/paradigm-shift/
[688] http://www.paradigmshiftcentral.com/
[689] http://www.paradigmshiftmagazine.com/
[690] http://consciouslifenews.com/shift-paradigm-global-awakening-includes-transformational-exercise/
[691] http://awakeningplanet.com/started-2-2/paradigm-shift/

Spiritual Awakening [692]

The Aquarius Paradigm [693]

The Awakening Shift [694]

The New Human Paradigm Shift [695]

The Paradigm Shift and How It Relates To Your Ascension [696]

The Secret of the Paradigm Shift [697]

Time For A Paradigm Shift [698]

What Is A Paradigm Shift? [699]

---

[692] http://www.cassandrasturdy.com/tag/spiritual-awakening
[693] http://aquariusparadigm.com/
[694] http://theawakeningshift.com/articles/
[695] http://thenewhumanconsciousness.blogspot.ca/
[696] http://lauraschwalm.wordpress.com/2014/01/03/the-paradigm-shift-and-how-it-relates-to-your-ascension/
[697] http://www.examiner.com/article/the-secret-of-the-paradigm-shift
[698] http://starseed-davina.com/time-paradigm-shift/
[699] http://www.taketheleap.com/define.html

Message 28

ESSENTIAL PRACTICES

Essential means [1] absolutely necessary; indispensable, [2] pertaining to, or constituting, the essence of something, [3] being such by its very <u>nature</u> or in the highest sense; natural; spontaneous: as in essential happiness.

In the words of Joseph Campbell ... *It's important to live life with the experience, and therefore the knowledge, of its mystery and of your own mystery. This gives life a new radiance, a new harmony, a new splendor. Thinking in mythological terms helps to put you in accord with the inevitable of this vale of tears. You learn to recognize the positive values in what appear to be the negative moments and aspects of your life. The big question is whether you are going to be able to say a hearty yes to your adventure.*

Jalaluddin Rumi, the great thirteenth-century Sufi mystic and poet, began his life as an orthodox Islamic believer.

However, he felt that to experience complete union with the divine, he needed to refrain from institutionalized religion and its prescribed form(s) of worship. [700]

With a message that continues to remains both profound, and yet simplistic, he shares that if you wish to affect the spirit, you must first make changes in the way your body responds to the world.

The following practices are absolutely essential to living life to the fullest.

In my frame of reference, so, too, do they constitute what it means to live an authentic life.

———————————————————— ❖ ————————————————————

---

[700]

http://www.dailyom.com/library/000/002/000002133.html

COMPASSION

When you are affected by the suffering of others, you are demonstrating compassion. Buddha and Jesus are the most well known exemplars of compassion.

The spiritual practice of compassion is often likened to the opening of the heart.

The practice of compassion (whereby you allow yourself to feel the suffering in the world, including your own, and then move toward that suffering with caring) increases one's capacity to care; so, too, does the practice of compassion reinforce charity and empathy.

While you may wish you could lessen another person's suffering, it is even more important that they experience those emotions, and resolve the conflict themselves, in order to learn.

Like a loving parent, all you can really do is empathize with them, understand the mistakes they make, and love them with all your being.

As an embodiment of compassion, you recognize that there is no separation between you and the person you are interacting with.

GRATITUDE

The cultivation of gratitude (which leads to increased happiness and positivity) is absolutely essential.

Experiencing gratitude is one of the most effective ways of getting in touch with your soul.

Gratitude takes you from limitation and fear (ego based) to expansion and love (heart based); you simply cannot operate on both levels at the same time.

Since ancient times, philosophers and sages from every spiritual tradition have taught that cultivating gratitude is a key to experiencing deeper levels of happiness, fulfillment, and well-being. [701]

One of the earliest advocates of a daily gratitude practice was Dutch philosopher Rabbi Baruch Spinoza.

---

[701] https://spiritualityhealth.com/articles/3-essential-practices-gratitude

In the seventeenth century, he suggested [702] that each day, for a month, we should ask ourselves the following three questions.

[1] Who or what inspired me today?

[2] What brought me happiness today?

[3] What brought me comfort and deep peace today?

The challenge of this journal practice becomes in *not* repeating answers from the previous entries.

I take the time to outline my answers in my Gratitude Journal. [703] [704] [705] [706] [707] [708]

---

[702] https://spiritualityhealth.com/articles/3-essential-practices-gratitude

[703] http://www.findinghappiness.com/gratitude-journal/

[704] http://www.lovely-life-plan.com/gratitude-journals.html

[705] http://calmmindwarmheart.com/gratitude-journal/

[706] http://www.positive-changes-coach.com/gratitude-journal.html

[707] http://www.creativeaffirmations.com/gratitude-journal.html

By acknowledging all of the goodness that we experience on a daily basis, so, too, are we inviting the universe to continue to bring us more of this same goodness.

In the words of Robert Louis Stevenson ... *There is no duty we so much underrate as the duty of being happy. By being happy we sow anonymous benefits upon the world.*

In the words of William Arthur Ward ... *Feeling gratitude and not expressing it is like wrapping a present and not giving it.* He also shares that ... *Gratitude can transform common days into thanksgivings, turn routine jobs into joy, and change ordinary opportunities into blessings.*

Keeping a Gratitude Journal helps to redirect the mind from negative thinking to positive thinking; hence, the more you concentrate on what is good in your life, the more positive and happy you feel.

---

[708] http://www.entheos.com/ideas/brian-johnson/1796/keep-a-gratitude-journal

In this way, it can be said that gratitude and well-being go hand-in-hand.

In the words of John F. Kennedy ... *As we express our gratitude, we must never forget that the highest appreciation is not to utter words, but to live by them.*

---

10 Ways to Become More Grateful [709]

10 Ways to Have a Happier Life, Part 1 [710]

10 Ways to Have a Happier Life, Part 2 [711]

17 Gratitude Prompting Questions [712]

---

[709]
http://greatergood.berkeley.edu/article/item/ten_ways_to_become_more_grateful1/

[710] http://www.huffingtonpost.com/andrew-weil-md/tips-for-a-happier-life_b_1071805.html

[711] http://www.drweil.com/drw/u/ART03235/10-Ways-to-Have-a-Happier-Life-Part-Two.html

[712] http://ripplerevolution.com/17-gratitude-prompting-questions-for-your-gratitude-journal/

Create and Maintain a Gratitude Journal for Life [713]

Evidence-Based Best Practices for Writing a Gratitude Journal [714] [715] [716]

Grateful 160 [717]

Gratitude 365 [718]

Gratitude Elevates Your Life to a Higher Frequency [719]

For Happiness, Keep a Gratitude Journal [720]

---

[713] http://happyrambles.com/

[714] http://cogsci.stackexchange.com/questions/5048/evidence-based-best-practices-for-writing-a-gratitude-journal

[715] http://www.healthcentral.com/anxiety/c/1443/164309/gratitude-journals/

[716] http://www.psychologytoday.com/blog/prefrontal-nudity/201211/the-grateful-brain

[717] http://grateful160.com/

[718] http://gratitude365app.com/

[719] http://www.huffingtonpost.com/oprah-winfrey/oprah-gratitude-thanksgiving_b_2171573.html

[720] http://www.everydayutilitarian.com/essays/for-happiness-keep-a-gratitude-journal/

How to Practice Gratitude [721]

How To Start A Gratitude Journal [722]

I Am Thankful [723]

Keeping a Gratitude Journal Can Change Your Perspective
[724]

Thank You Notes: Gratitude Examples [725]

The 31 Benefits of Gratitude [726]

---

[721]

http://www.gratefulness.org/readings/practice_gratitude.htm
[722] http://www.clarejosa.com/featured/how-to-start-a-gratitude-journal-how-to-choose-which-of-the-3-levels-you-want-to-take-it-to/
[723] http://www.iamthankful.com/gratitude-journal/users/register
[724]

http://www.yummymummyclub.ca/family/mummy/20130314/how-keeping-a-gratitude-journal-can-change-your-perspective
[725] http://www.buzzle.com/articles/thank-you-notes-gratitude-examples.html
[726] http://happierhuman.com/benefits-of-gratitude/

The Gratitude Journal Project [727]

The New Science of Gratitude [728]

The Power of Gratitude [729] [730]

The Transformative Power of Gratitude [731]

Tips for Keeping a Gratitude Journal [732]

Today I Am Grateful For [733]

---

[727] http://thegratitudejournalproject.blogspot.ca/
[728] http://gratitudepower.net/science.htm
[729] http://www.oprah.com/spirit/The-Power-of-Gratitude
[730] http://gaicomans.com/2013/08/06/the-power-of-daily-gratitude/
[731] http://www.beliefnet.com/Wellness/Gratitude/The-Transformative-Power-Of-Gratitude.aspx
[732]

http://greatergood.berkeley.edu/article/item/tips_for_keeping_a_gratitude_journal
[733] http://www.learnmyself.com/Start-Gratitude-Journal

INTEGRITY

When we have armed ourselves with what we believe to be our truths, to the best of our ability, we must learn to live those truths with integrity.

We have to *mean what we say.*

We also have to be willing to *live what we believe.*

Living with integrity also means we have to be willing to *listen to our heart.*

There will be times when what we hold to be true in our intellect is in conflict with the deeper wisdom of our heart.

This is when we must to be willing to re-examine those beliefs; if needed, so, too, must we be willing to replace those staid, and outdated, beliefs with those that resonate with the wisdom of the heart.

Our *actions always reflect* our *true beliefs and values.*

If ever our actions make us uncomfortable, this becomes the time when we must be willing to demonstrate the courage and integrity to carefully examine who we are and what it is that we really believe.

LAUGHTER

Laughter is an excellent way of cleansing the body through the release of stress.

Paul E. McGhee (Ph.D.) shares that ... *Your sense of humor is one of the most powerful tools you have to make certain that your daily mood and emotional state support good health.*

In working with the Law of Attraction, so, too, do we know that the key secret to becoming a deliberate (conscious) creator is to *feel good.*

According to e. e. cummings ... *The most wasted of all days is one without laughter.*

According to Mark Twain ... *Against the assault of laughter, nothing can stand.*

Health Benefits of Laughter [734] [735]

Laughter and Health [736] [737]

Laughter is The Best Medicine [738]

Stress Relief from Laughter [739]

The Benefits of Laughter [740]

The Connection Between Laughter, Humor and Good Health [741]

---

[734] http://www.care2.com/greenliving/8-health-benefits-of-laughter.html

[735] http://life.gaiam.com/article/7-benefits-laughter

[736] http://healthpsych.psy.vanderbilt.edu/laughter.htm

[737] http://www.huffingtonpost.ca/2012/07/23/laughter-and-health_n_1695214.html

[738] http://www.helpguide.org/life/humor_laughter_health.htm

[739] http://www.mayoclinic.org/stress-relief/art-20044456

[740] http://www.psychologytoday.com/articles/200304/the-benefits-laughter

[741] http://www2.ca.uky.edu/hes/fcs/factshts/hsw-caw-807.pdf

LETTING GO (GETTING OUT OF OUR OWN WAY)

Letting go is not about holding onto things that we think we need.

Letting go is about developing the ability to cope with change, to be flexible, to simplify your life.

Letting go is about freedom from limitations, distractions, complications.

Letting go is about developing flexibility and openness.

Letting go is about allowing life to unfold with grace.

———————◆◇◆———————

It was Mahatma Gandhi who said that ... *Our greatness lies not so much in being able to remake the world as being able to remake ourselves.*

6 Ways To Allow Life To Unfold [742]

7 Essential Steps to Get Out of Your Own Way [743]

Are You Having Trouble Letting Go? [744]

Detox Yourself of These 5 BS Belief Systems [745]

Getting Out Of Our Own Way [746]

<u>Getting Out Of Our Own Way: Love Is The Only Answer</u> (Michele Doucette) [747] [748]

---

[742] http://www.vishnusvirtues.com/how-to-manifest-your-hearts-desires-without-shaking-down-the-universe-like-a-mob-boss/

[743] http://onewithnow.com/7-essential-steps-to-get-out-of-your-own-way/

[744] http://www.applythelawofattraction.com/lettinggo-law-attraction/

[745] http://www.thelawofattraction.com/detox-yourself-of-these-5-b-belief-systems/

[746] http://creatingspace365.com/2013/03/26/090-getting-out-of-our-own-way/

[747] http://www.amazon.com/Getting-Out-Our-Own-Way/dp/1935786245/

[748] http://www.amazon.ca/Getting-Out-Our-Own-Way/dp/1935786245/

How Letting Go Gets You What You Need [749]

Is Your Ego Getting In The Way? [750]

Letting Go [751] [752]

Letting Go For The Life You Want [753]

The 20 Things You Need To Let Go To Be Happy [754]

The Secret of Letting Go (Guy Finley) [755]

The S.T.A.R.R. of Letting Go [756]

---

[749] http://scottwesterman.com/?p=2576

[750] http://advancedlifeskills.com/blog/personal-development-%E2%80%93-is-your-ego-getting-in-the-way/

[751] http://drlwilson.com/articles/letting_go.htm

[752] http://saltspringcentre.com/2013/09/letting-go/

[753] http://life.gaiam.com/article/letting-go-life-you-want

[754] http://elitedaily.com/life/20s-things-you-need-to-let-go-to-live-happy-life/

[755] http://www.guyfinley.org/store/books-and-ebooks/317

[756] http://www.positivelypositive.com/2012/08/19/the-s-t-a-r-r-of-letting-go/

MEDITATION

Meditation is a practice in which an individual trains the mind or induces a mode of consciousness, either to realize some benefit or as an end in itself.

Buddhist Meditation [757]

Evidence Shows Transcendental Meditation Has Real Health Benefits [758]

Free Guided Meditation [759]

Free Meditation [760]

---

[757] http://www.wildmind.org/
[758] http://www.huffingtonpost.com/robert-schneider/evidence-shows-transcendental-meditation-has-real-health-benefits_b_4747436.html
[759] http://marc.ucla.edu/body.cfm?id=22
[760] http://www.freemeditation.com/

Golden Rule Meditation Exercises [761]

How to Meditate [762]

Is Meditation The New Antidepressant? [763]

Learning Meditation [764]

Meditation [765] [766] [767]

Meditation and Mental Culture [768]

Meditation: An Introduction [769]

---

[761]

https://www.scarboromissions.ca/Golden_rule/meditation_exercises.php

[762] http://www.how-to-meditate.org/

[763] http://life.nationalpost.com/2014/01/13/is-meditation-the-new-anti-depressant-mindfulness-practice-may-be-more-effective-than-drugs-for-anxiety-depression/

[764] http://www.learningmeditation.com/

[765]

http://www.beliefnet.com/Wellness/Meditation/index.aspx

[766] http://www.mayoclinic.org/meditation/art-20045858

[767] http://www.psychologytoday.com/basics/meditation

[768] http://dharma.ncf.ca/introduction/meditation.html

[769] http://nccam.nih.gov/health/meditation/overview.htm

Meditation 101: The Neuroscience of Why Meditation Works [770]

Meditation Center [771]

Meditation In Action [772]

Meditation Oasis [773]

Meditation Timers [774] [775]

Open Source Meditation [776]

Osho Meditation [777]

---

[770] http://www.huffingtonpost.com/ashley-turner/how-meditation-works_b_4702629.html?utm_hp_ref=healthy-living
[771] http://www.meditationcenter.com/
[772] http://www.shinzen.org/
[773] https://www.meditationoasis.com/
[774] http://www.the-guided-meditation-site.com/online-meditation-timer.html
[775] http://www.insightmeditationcenter.org/meditation-timers/
[776] http://meditation.org.au/index.asp?mobilecheck=true
[777] http://www.osho.com/meditate

Project Meditation® [778]

Sufi Meditation Center [779]

The Art of Meditation (AOM) [780]

The Chopra Center [781] [782]

The Guided Meditation Site [783]

The Meditation Podcast [784]

The Transcendental Meditation Program [785]

Transcendental Meditation® Technique [786]

---

[778] http://www.project-meditation.org/
[779] http://www.sufimeditationcenter.com/
[780] http://www.artofmeditation.com/
[781] https://chopracentermeditation.com/
[782] http://www.chopra.com/ccl-
meditation/index.html#fragment-1
[783] http://www.the-guided-meditation-site.com/
[784] http://www.themeditationpodcast.com/
[785] http://www.maharishi.ca/
[786] http://www.tm.org/

MINDFULNESS

Mindfulness refers to being fully attentive and aware (without judgment) in the present moment, whereas meditation involves engaging in a mental exercise (concentration on one's breathing or repetition of a mantra) for spiritual or relaxation purposes.

Based on the concept of mindfulness [787] in Buddhist meditation, it becomes through mindfulness practice that we can learn to be less reactive and more intentional in both words as well as actions.

———————×———————

Benefits of Mindfulness [788]

Mindfulness [789] [790] [791]

———————

[787] http://en.wikipedia.org/wiki/Mindfulness
[788] http://www.helpguide.org/harvard/mindfulness.htm
[789] http://www.psychologytoday.com/basics/mindfulness
[790] http://dharma.ncf.ca/introduction/instructions/sati.html
[791] http://www.get.gg/mindfulness.htm

Mindfulness Exercises [792]

Mindfulness Without Borders [793]

The Centre for Mindfulness Studies [794]

The Four Foundations of Mindfulness [795]

The Mindfulness Bell [796]

The Mindfulness Information Website [797]

The Mindfulness Institute [798]

UCLA Mindful Awareness Research Center [799]

---

[792] http://youth.anxietybc.com/mindfulness-exercises
[793] http://mindfulnesswithoutborders.org/
[794] http://www.mindfulnessstudies.com/
[795] http://www.arrowriver.ca/dhamma/founMind.html
[796] http://www.iamhome.org/
[797] http://www.mindfulnet.org/
[798] http://www.mindfulnessbasedlearning.com/
[799] http://marc.ucla.edu/

What is Mindfulness? [800] [801]

800

http://greatergood.berkeley.edu/topic/mindfulness/definition
[801] http://www.wildmind.org/applied/daily-life/what-is-mindfulness

THE FOUR NOBLE TRUTHS

The spiritual path of Buddhism begins with the Four Noble Truths; not only the most basic Buddhist teachings, it is said that they encompass all of the teachings of the Buddha.

Within the Truths are woven the Buddhist understanding of the self, of karma and rebirth, and of enlightenment and Nirvana.

It is said that wisdom and compassion are the two eyes of Buddhism.

The fourth noble truth is the eightfold path, meaning that it is the means by which enlightenment may be realized.

The historical Buddha first explained the Eightfold Path in his first sermon after his enlightenment, preserved in the Dhammacakkappavattana Sutta. [802] [803]

802

http://en.wikipedia.org/wiki/Dhammacakkappavattana_Sutta
[803] http://www.ancient-buddhist-texts.net/English-Texts/Earliest-Discourses/index.htm

Basics of Buddhism [804]

The Four Noble Truths [805] [806] [807] [808] [809] [810] [811] [812] [813] [814]

The Nobility of the Truths [815]

---

[804] http://www.pbs.org/edens/thailand/buddhism.htm

[805] http://www.buddhanet.net/4noble.htm

[806] http://viewonbuddhism.org/4_noble_truths.html

[807]
http://www.bbc.co.uk/religion/religions/buddhism/beliefs/fournobletruths_1.shtml

[808] http://www.school-for-champions.com/religion/buddhism_four_noble_truths.htm#.Uva3EuSYZ9A

[809]
http://www.lamayeshe.com/index.php?sect=article&id=380

[810] http://www.age-of-the-sage.org/buddhism/buddha_teachings.html

[811]
http://www.buddhamind.info/leftside/under/buddha/4truths.htm

[812] http://www.accesstoinsight.org/lib/study/truths.html

[813]
http://www.geocities.com/lesliebarclay/FourNobleTruths.html

[814] http://www.souledout.org/wesak/4nobletruths.html

SPIRITUAL PRACTICES

Practices for the body = yoga postures, Tai Chi, Qigong, breathing exercises, energy balancing, dance.

Practices for the mind = meditation, contemplation, stillness, mindfulness, repetition of mantras, study of spiritual teachings, hypnosis, guided imagery, affirmations, gratitude, expressing yourself.

Practices for the spirit = prayer, chanting, drumming, song, loving kindness, communing with nature.

Center for Spiritual Intelligence [816]

Essential Teachings and Practices of Spiritual Science [817]

---

[815] http://www.accesstoinsight.org/lib/authors/bodhi/bps-essay_20.html

[816] http://spiritualintelligence.com/

[817] https://www.vesica.org/spiritual-science/spiritual-science-articles/29-online-courses/96-essential-teachings-and-practices-of-spiritual-science

How is the Body Essential to Spiritual Evolution? [818]

Integral Life Practice Kit [819]

Integral Spiritual Practice [820]

Rumi's Four Essential Practices [821]

Spiritual Wellness [822]

The Essence of Wicca Spirituality [823]

The Essential Practice for a Spiritual Life [824]

---

[818] http://www.elephantjournal.com/2013/07/how-is-the-body-essential-to-spiritual-evolution/

[819] http://myilp.com/teleseminar/ILP_Book_Preview.pdf

[820] http://www.terrypatten.com/integral-spiritual-practice

[821] http://www.muebooks.com/rumis-four-essential-practices-PDF-704900/

[822] http://wellness.ucr.edu/spiritual_wellness.html

[823] http://www.wicca-spirituality.com/wicca-spirituality.html

[824] http://edmundians.blogspot.ca/2008/10/essential-practice-for-spiritual-life.html

The Essential Practice of Body Prayer [825]

The Essential Practice of Radical Acceptance [826]

The Koan of Breathing [827]

The Most Essential Spiritual Practice [828]

---

[825]

http://www.patheos.com/blogs/spiritualdirection101/2013/0
7/the-essential-practice-of-body-prayer/

[826]

http://www.patheos.com/blogs/spiritualdirection101/2013/0
7/the-essential-practice-of-radical-acceptance/

[827] http://www.beliefnet.com/Faiths/Buddhism/Articles/The-
Koan-of-Breathing.aspx?p=1

[828]

http://www.truedivinenature.com/EssentialSpiritualPractice.
htm

Message 29

THE LAW OF ATTRACTION

Abraham says … *When you give your attention to a subject and feel only positive emotion about it … it will come very quickly into your experience.*

This is the premise behind creative visualization.

Belief is what makes abundance creation possible; this can be further fostered by using visualization techniques.

When you picture something in your mind's eye, it starts to take shape.

As you add colour and impeccable detail, using all of your bodily senses, it becomes real (tangible).

Abraham Hicks Publications [829] is the original source material for the current *Law of Attraction* wave that is sweeping the world; the 21st century inspiration for thousands of books, films, essays and lectures that are responsible for the current paradigm shift in consciousness.

Apply the Law of Attraction [830]

Basic Law of Attraction Practitioner Certification [831]

Basic Law of Attraction Wealth Practitioner Certification [832]

Deliberate Receiving Blog [833]

Ensure Your Dream Life With The Law of Attraction [834]

---

[829] http://www.abraham-hicks.com/lawofattractionsource/index.php
[830] http://www.applythelawofattraction.com/
[831] http://www.loatraining.com/
[832] http://www.trainforwealth.com/
[833] http://www.deliberateblog.com/
[834] http://www.psitek.net/pages/PsiTek-ensure-your-dream-life-with-the-law-of-attraction-Contents.html#gsc.tab=0

God and The Law of Attraction (Carol Tuttle) [835]

Jesus Taught It Too (The Early Roots of The Law of Attraction) [836]

Law of Attraction Magazine [837]

Law of Attraction Principles [838] [839]

Law of Attraction Radio Network [840]

Law of Attraction Resource Guide [841]

Mind Movies (multi-media visualization tool) [842]

Powerful Intentions: The Law of Attraction Community [843]

---

[835] http://liveyourtruth.com/en/god-and-the-law-of-attraction
[836] http://www.psitek.net/pages/PsiTek-jesus-taught-it-too-Contents.html#gsc.tab=0
[837] http://lawofattractionmag.com/
[838] http://www.essential-practices.com/
[839] http://www.essential-practices.com/law-of-attraction.html
[840] http://loaradionetwork.com/
[841] http://www.lawofattraction-resourceguide.com/
[842] http://www.mindmovies.com/?10107
[843] http://www.powerfulintentions.org/

The 11 Forgotten Laws [844]

The Cosmic Law of Attraction [845]

The Hidden Power of Universal Laws [846]

The Law of Attraction [847] [848] [849] [850]

The Law of Attraction (Steve Pavlina) [851]

The Law of Attraction and A Course in Miracles [852]

---

[844] http://www.the11forgottenlaws.com/
[845] http://www.one-mind-one-energy.com/cosmic-law-of-attraction.html
[846] http://www.psitek.net/pages/PsiTek-the-hidden-power-of-universal-laws-Contents.html#gsc.tab=0
[847] http://www.thelawofattraction.com/
[848] http://www.thelawofattraction.com/what-is-the-law-of-attraction/
[849] http://www.presentlove.com/law-of-attraction/
[850] http://www.wellbeingalignment.com/law-of-attraction.html#sthash.QfFblolC.dpbs
[851] http://www.stevepavlina.com/blog/2006/08/the-law-of-attraction/
[852] http://acimexplained.com/the-law-of-attraction-and-a-course-in-miracles/

The Law of Attraction Library [853]

The Law of Attraction Network [854]

The Law of Attraction Revisited [855]

The Law of Attraction: Take Control of Your Life [856]

The Law of Attraction Key [857]

The Real Secret to the Law of Attraction [858]

The Secret to Living the Law of Attraction [859]

Thought Vibration (William Walker Atkinson) [860]

---

[853] http://www.thelawofattraction.org/
[854] http://thelawofattractionnetworks.ning.com/
[855] http://www.psychologytoday.com/blog/the-blame-game/201401/the-law-attraction-revisited
[856] http://www.highexistence.com/law-of-attraction/
[857] http://www.lawofattractionkey.com/
[858] http://johnassaraf.com/law-of-attraction/the-real-secret-to-the-law-of-attraction
[859] http://www.thesecrettolivingthelawofattraction.com/
860

http://newthoughtlibrary.com/atkinsonWilliam/thoughtVibration/

Conscious Creation

A CONSCIOUS CREATOR STARTS BY LETTING GO.

THE KEY SECRET TO BECOMING A DELIBERATE (CONSCIOUS) CREATOR IS TO <u>FEEL GOOD</u>.

PERCEPTION IS CREATION, MEANING THAT I AM THE CREATOR OF MY EXPERIENCE.

MY WORDS ARE THE TOOLS THROUGH WHICH I CREATE.

CONSCIOUS CREATORS LIVE FROM THE HEART.

There are a great many individuals who are unconscious creators (creating by default), wanting to remain confined to their levels of comfort and security.

By comparison, you are here to learn to become a conscious creator, creating by way of deliberate choice.

How, then, does one define a conscious creator?

A conscious creator spends his (her) energy focusing only on what he (she) wants, not pushing against what he (she) does not want; this means that what he (she) does not want does not even capture his (her) attention, because that would be giving power to a reality that he (she) does not desire. [861]

A conscious creator does not need to speak or act in negative ways; there may be times, however, when he (she) needs to express negative emotions, but solely for the purpose of releasing them. [862]

A conscious creator makes the same choice, over and over again, as the powerful act of a peaceful warrior (someone who chooses to focus on what he (she) wants rather than fight the world). [863]

---

[861] http://www.essential-practices.com/conscious-creator.html
[862] Ibid.
[863] Ibid.

A conscious creator looks for opportunities to clarify his (her) focus; even if someone claims an untruth, a conscious creator allows this, claiming a higher truth within him (her) self. [864] This gives him (her) the power to pursue his (her) vision without being deflated or influenced by those who protest something else. [865]

A conscious creator trusts in his (her) understanding of who he (she) really is and the process of attracting what he (she) wants. [866]

---

3 Important Ways to Boost Your Energy as a Conscious Creator [867]

Access Consciousness [868]

---

[864] http://www.essential-practices.com/conscious-creator.html
[865] Ibid.
[866] Ibid.
[867] http://carimurphy.com/archives/3484
[868] http://www.accessconsciousness.com/

Are You a Conscious Creator? [869]

Becoming A Deliberate Creator [870]

Becoming Conscious Co-Creators of Reality [871] [872]

Be The Conscious Creator [873]

Conscious Creation [874]

Conscious Creator Imagery [875]

---

[869] http://keystothemind.com/are-you-a-conscious-creator/
[870] http://www.calmdownmind.com/becoming-a-deliberate-creator/
[871] http://www.trans4mind.com/counterpoint/index-life-purpose/page10.shtml
[872]

http://beyourdream.empowernetwork.com/blog/becoming-a-conscious-creato
[873] http://carnegieworld.blogspot.ca/2007/12/be-conscious-creator.html
[874]

http://www.innerawakeningsonline.com/articles/conscious-creation/
[875] http://www.timothyernster.com/conscious-creator-imagery/

Conscious Mastery [876]

Conscious Shift Co-Creator Radio Network [877]

Conscious Thinking Oath [878]

Conscious Wealth Institute [879]

Creative Manifesting [880]

Do You Know the Path of the Peaceful Warrior? [881]

How to Become a Conscious Creator [882]

---

[876] http://consciousmastery.org/what-is-conscious-mastery/
[877] http://www.co-creatornetwork.com/hosts/consciousshift/host_bio.htm
[878] http://www.define-your-purpose-in-life.com/conscious_thinking_2.html
[879] http://consciouswealthinstitute.com/
[880] http://www.creatavision.com/
[881] http://www.activistpost.com/2013/07/do-you-know-path-of-peaceful-warrior.html
[882] http://www.melanietoniaevans.com/articles/laws-of-life.htm

If the Creator Were Conscious of Himself [883]

Lessons Learned from Peaceful Warrior [884]

Master the Path of the Peaceful Warrior (course with Dan Millman) [885]

Mind Reality (Enoch Tan) [886]

Path of the Peaceful Warrior [887]

Teaching Your Child To Become Conscious Creators [888]

---

[883] http://carljungdepthpsychology.blogspot.ca/2012/02/if-creator-were-conscious-of.html
[884] http://sourcesofinsight.com/lessons-learned-from-peaceful-warrior/
[885] http://www.dailyom.com/cgi-bin/courses/courseoverview.cgi?cid=160
[886] http://www.enochtan.com/
[887] http://edelomahony.com/2011/03/20/in-being-a-conscious-creator/
[888] http://www.finerminds.com/consciousness-awareness/teaching-children-law-of-attraction-2/

Ten Ways To Fail As A Conscious Creator [889]

The 7 Habits of A Conscious Creator [890]

The 12 Dimensions of Creation [891]

The Creators Code [892]

The Conscious Creator Forum [893] [894]

The Conscious Creator: Six Laws For Manifesting Your Masterpiece Life (Kris Kohn and Stephen Palmer) [895] [896] [897]

---

[889] http://voices.yahoo.com/ten-ways-fail-as-conscious-creator-understanding-43587.html

[890] http://innerarchitect.wordpress.com/2008/04/25/the-7-habits-of-a-conscious-creator-think-your-way-to-a-new-you/

[891] http://www.bibliotecapleyades.net/ciencia/ciencia_dimensiones01.htm

[892] http://www.creatorscode.com/

[893] http://realtalkworld.com/2013/06/29/the-conscious-creator-forum/

[894] http://www.thomhartmann.com/users/worldchangeguy/blog/2013/06/conscious-creator-forum

[895] http://agatheringofexperts.com/kris-krohn/

The Conscious Mind [898]

The Peaceful Warrior's Way (Dan Millman) [899]

Thought Mastery Program [900]

We Are The Creators Of The World [901]

What Conscious Creators Know [902]

What Does It Mean To Be A Conscious Creator? [903]

---

[896] http://self.gutenberg.org/eBooks/WPLBN0002827589-Conscious-Creator-by-Krohn--Kris.aspx?&Trail=collection&Words=

[897] http://www.amazon.com/exec/obidos/ASIN/0985967706/portalsofspirit

[898] http://www.abundance-and-happiness.com/the-conscious-mind.html

[899] http://www.peacefulwarrior.com/

[900] http://www.frederickzappone.com/

[901] http://paulbassler.com/

[902] http://www.dreammanifesto.com/personal-power-what-conscious-creators-know.html

[903] http://imagi-creation.com/articles/english/what-does-it-mean-to-be-a-conscious-creator/

Yet More Evidence Emerges That Our Universe Is A Grand Simulation Created By An Intelligent Designer [904]

904

http://divinitynow.com/038985_universe_simulation_intelligent_design.html

Creative Visualization

The future is created by the thoughts that you think.

In keeping, your thoughts are always driven by the core beliefs that you hold.

If you want the future to be better, you need to think thoughts that make you feel better.

Visualization is the process of using your thoughts and emotions to imagine, and then attract, the people, circumstances, situations and opportunities you most desire into your life.

Napoleon Hill has been talking about it for nearly a hundred years and it has been regularly used, for decades, by people from all walks of life, to achieve their goals in a much faster and easier way.

A Harvard Medical School study found that subjects who visualized themselves practicing the piano had the same structural changes in the brain as those who actually participated in the intense practical piano training sessions.

The secret to effective visualization is two-fold.

[1] You must first create a clear mental picture of what you want.

[2] You must then visualize yourself achieving these results with feeling and emotion.

Visualization (or creative visualization as some term it) simply involves learning to use your imagination to create clear visual images, ideas or feelings (through sensing) in a more conscious way; as one continues to focus on the image (idea, feeling) in a positive way, the energy results in the creation of that imagined reality.

What you focus on, you attract.

We live in a quantum sea of vibrating energy; an incredible energy that is always responding to how we think (feel, believe) and what we think (feel, believe).

Our thoughts and feelings are creative forces.

Even though the subconscious mind cannot distinguish between what is real and what is imagined, it will act upon the images that you create, whether they reflect your current reality or not.

This is where visualization comes into play.

There is a mental trick to visualization; you need to live and feel as if you *already have* what you want.

As long as you continue to persist in your vision, you will achieve what you want.

Visualization is one of the most significant keys to success.

253

Actively picturing yourself achieving a goal will help you actually achieve it.

Visualization + Emotion + Repetition + Inspired Action = Abundance

When you visualize, you must see (hear, feel, smell, taste, touch) everything in vivid detail, taking the time to spend at least 15 minutes each day engaged thusly.

You *need* to be able to envision your dream. When you take the time to visualize, the things you are imagining seem to be magnetically drawn to you.

Napoleon Hill, author of <u>Think and Grow Rich,</u> has this to say … *Our brains become magnetized with the dominating thoughts we hold in our minds, and, by means with which no man is familiar, these 'magnets' attract to us the forces, the people, the circumstances of life which harmonize with the nature of our dominating thoughts.*

Our mind and thoughts produce energy.

Energy always follows thought and feeling.

Thoughts are always birthed in the spiritual realm, first, before they are reproduced in the manifested physical realm of our existence.

Visualization, then, changes you physically, energetically and spiritually in that you are affected on all three levels *anytime you imagine with feeling.*

I like to avail of the **EVERYDAY VISUALIZATION SYSTEM** [905] created by my good friend Carl Harvey.

As a Master Practitioner of NLP, Carl has discovered that the fastest way to generate results involves using visualization combined with NLP; hence, his *five-step formula* systematic system.

---

[905] http://www.portalsofspirit.com/creative-visualization/

This program also includes a collection of 13 guided visualization MP3 audio files, training videos as well as several other powerful audio files.

Carl literally takes you by the hand and shows you exactly how to use his *five-step formula* systematic system to easily (and quickly) create powerful visualizations that get big results.

Relaxing deep into the Alpha state (as per Carl's program) is what gives you better access to your subconscious mind.

You need to create a sensory rich image of what you want to experience; sights, sounds and feelings are particularly important avenues.

You need to envision each goal as vividly as you can; as you see it happening in your mind's eye, making it as real as you can, for this is what builds expectation.

You must believe it will happen, just as you have imagined it.

You must expect it to happen, just as you have imagined it.

You must trust it to happen, just as you have imagined it.

The more you trust the process, the faster your desire will find you.

I also make use of the guided visualizations that have already been created, by Carl, as per his **8 MINUTE MANIFESTING** [906] program; a collection of 20 MP3 audio files that combine brainwave entrainment, NLP, hypnosis and guided visualization; the single most effective way to get results.

One of the common misconceptions about visualization is that you need to be a master at "seeing" crystal-clear images inside your imagination; this is simply not true.

The process is all about *how good the visualization feels*, not how it looks.

---

[906] http://www.portalsofspirit.com/creative-visualization-2/

In fact, *the key is to generate the positive emotions you expect to experience* when you manifest your goal. Paradoxically, this seems to attract opportunities, people and circumstances to you.

As you spend time visualizing each day, you will begin to feel an emotional shift, the cue that you have been waiting for; this is the sign that you are now broadcasting a new vibrational signal. The longer you are able to hold this new vibration, the faster your reality will shift.

As already eluded to, there are three necessary elements to successful visualization.

DESIRE = *I have the desire to create* what I have hereby chosen to visualize.

BELIEF = *I believe in my goal and have the confidence that I will achieve it (or something better).*

ACCEPTANCE = *I accept my vision and will continue to pursue it with the full intention of bringing it to fruition.*

If we always get from life what we think about, take the time to follow (and work towards achieving) the following suggestions.

►Refuse to accept limiting beliefs.

►Work on eliminating limiting beliefs.

►Visualize your dream in vivid, sensory rich detail.

Knowing that your subconscious cannot tell the difference between a real memory and a vividly imagined one, take the time to use all of your senses when you visualize.

See what you will see.

Hear what you will hear.

Feel how good it feels to have everything you dream of, and more, in an easy and relaxed manner, in a healthy and positive way.

Here is what Jack Canfield has to say about visualization.

If we can believe in some of the newer theories of quantum physics, visualizing your desires will send out waves of energy that will attract the people and resources to you that you need to accomplish your goals.

Here is what Bob Proctor, creator of <u>The Science of Getting Rich</u> has to share about visualization.

When you hold the image of your goal on the screen of your mind, in the present tense, you are vibrating in harmony with every particle of energy necessary for the manifestation of your image on the physical plane.

By holding that image, those particles of energy are moving toward you (attraction) and you are moving toward them, because that is the law.

It also needs to be shared that my good friend Carl Harvey has this to add to Bob's words.

The ability to hold the image of what you want probably isn't enough for you to manifest it.

Yes, you should do everything you can to stimulate an intense, burning desire for whatever you want to create, manifest and experience more of.

You should certainly visualize every day, because in time you will rid yourself of ideas of lack and scarcity, growing more confident.

But the real keystone to manifesting is not simply holding a vision of what you want.

It is BELIEF.

Possessing a deep, self belief is as rare and compelling as a bird of paradise. REAL belief is attractive, magnetic, and almost impossible to resist.

Having Belief is what attracts the "magic" of synchronicity and flow.

Holographic Creation

According to Christopher Westra, Holographic Creation is the process of spiritually pre-creating reality by building a light matrix (or hologram) out of the electromagnetic spectrum. [907] In keeping, you can holographically create events, situations, and things through the focused imaginative powers of your mind.

He also offers a Ten Lesson Mini-Course [908] whereby the topics include ......

[1] What Exactly is Holographic Creation?

[2] Five Personal Benefits you receive from Holographic Manifesting

[3] The Mind Expanding Power of Extreme Visualization

---

[907] http://lightisreal.com/holographiccreation.html
[908] http://icreatereality.com/

[4] Exactly Where Does Your Creative Power Come From?

[5] The Gunnison Three Kick Rule, or "Will I Pay the Price?"

[6] The Single Major Manifesting Mistake that Prevents Success

[7] The Second Major Manifesting Mistake People Commonly Make

[8] Three Types of Manifestors: Which One Are You?

[9] How to Manifest Money (Comes with Free Money Meditation MP3)

[10] The Two Most Powerful Ways of Changing Beliefs

Ten Ways that Holographic Creation is More Powerful than Visualization [909]

---

[909] http://lightisreal.com/HolographicCreation.pdf

Christopher has two PDF files that explore Holographic Creation in vivid detail.

I Create Reality: Beyond Visualization (Christopher Westra) [910]

Realms of Joy, Time of Light: How You Can Master Holographic Time (Christopher Westra) [911]

As A Man Thinketh by James Allen (updated version) [912]

Holographic Belief Replacement [913]

Manifesting Resources to Spread the Light [914]

---

[910]

http://www.federaljack.com/ebooks/Spirituality/holocreation.pdf

[911] http://www.icreatereality.com/HolographicTime.pdf

[912]

http://asamanthinkethnewversion.com/AsAManThinkethNewVersion1.pdf

[913] http://holographicbeliefreplacement.com/

[914] http://lightisreal.com/index.html

Online Holographic Creation Sheet [915]

Ten Laws of Attraction [916]

Using Your Holographic Mind [917]

---

[915] http://holographiccreationsheet.com/
[916] http://www.trans4mind.com/LawsofAttraction.pdf
[917] http://meta-wealth.com/applications/using-your-holographic-mind/

Message 30

THE INTENTION EXPERIMENT

The Intention Experiment is a series of scientifically controlled, web-based experiments testing the power of intention to change the physical world.

Thousands of volunteers from 30 countries around the world have participated in Intention Experiments thus far; in summation, this is the largest mind over matter experiment in history.

Healing Intention Experiments (George Noory) [918]

How The Power of Intention Alters Matter [919]

---

[918] http://www.coasttocoastam.com/shows/2012/06/06
[919] http://www.spiritofmaat.com/archive/mar2/tiller.htm

Intention Experiments [920]

Living the Field course (Lynne McTaggart) [921]

Lynne McTaggart [922]

The Intention Experiment (Lynne McTaggart) [923]

The Intention Experiment: Where The Lost Symbol's Fiction Becomes Fact [924]

The Intention Workbook (Lynne McTaggart) [925]

---

[920] http://www.psyleron.com/info/research/intention.html
[921] http://theintentionexperiment.com/start-adventure
[922] http://www.lynnemctaggart.com/
[923] http://theintentionexperiment.com/
[924] http://life.gaiam.com/article/intention-experiment-where-lost-symbols-fiction-becomes-fact
[925]

http://www.healingwiththemasters.com/LynneSpecial/pdfs/Lynn-CM-IntentionWorkbookNew.pdf

Pelmanism

Invented by William Joseph Ennever, Pelmanism involves memory games and attention-training techniques.

Some resemble what present-day practitioners call mindfulness; others embody the currently popular idea of willpower as a trainable muscle. [926]

Mind and Memory [927]

The Original Pelmanism Course (FREE) [928]

The Pelman School of Memory [929]

926

http://www.theguardian.com/lifeandstyle/2012/aug/31/change-life-pelmanism-mind-trainning

[927] https://archive.org/details/mindmemorypelman00pelm

[928] http://www.sector51.com/

[929] http://www.ennever.com/histories/history386p.php

Neville Goddard

Neville Goddard was the fourth child born to Joseph Nathaniel Goddard and Wilhelmina (née Hinkinson) Goddard on February 19, 1905 in St. Michael, Barbados (the British West Indies). He had nine siblings; eight brothers and one sister.

In 1922, at the age of seventeen, he came to the United States to study drama. During this time, he became a dancer and formed a dance company. He met and married his first wife; they had a son, Joseph Neville Goddard.

While on tour with his dance company in England, he developed an interest in metaphysics. When he came back to New York, he gave up theater and devoted his attention to the study of mystical and spiritual matters.

In 1931, Neville met Abdullah, an Ethiopian-born Jewish Rabbi. With Abdullah, he studied the Kabala, a Jewish form of mysticism, and obtained illuminating insights into the books of the Bible.

269

It was Abdullah who taught Neville [1] how to use the law of consciousness and [2] how to see the Bible from a psychological perspective.

To give credence to Neville's view would be to go against the teachings of organized religion for thousands of years, and yet many new philosophical thinkers of the late 1800s to the early 20th century (Wallace Wattles, Napoleon Hill, Geneviève Behrend, Thomas Troward) all believed the same: *as man creates things from his mind, this, then, makes him God.*

In the 1930s, he met and married his second wife; they had a daughter, Victoria Goddard.

Neville traveled widely throughout the United States, eventually settling in Los Angeles where he made his home.

In 1943, at the age of 38, he was drafted into the U.S army. A few weeks into the training, he was honorably discharged.

During the 1950s, he gave talks both on television and radio.

In addition, he spent many years of his life giving lectures at the Wilshire Ebell Theater. Most of his lectures were confined to Los Angeles, San Francisco and New York in the 1960s and early 1970s.

Neville based his early lectures and books on a technique of creating your reality through your imagination (calling this technique the Law).

He would often describe the Law by relating how he made a sea voyage from New York to Barbados to see his family during the depression, yet had no money of his own.

In addition, he also related how he was honorably discharged from the United States military service in order for him to continue his lectures through the use of imaginary power.

Neville urged people to learn how to use their imaginary power, lovingly on behalf of others, for man was moving into a world where everything was to become subject to his imaginary power.

In 1959, Neville Goddard began to apply what he called the Promise.

During the late 1960s and early 1970s, he began to place more emphasis on the Promise as compared to the Law, mainly because he had come to view the use of imaginary power to change a certain circumstance as temporary.

Neville departed from this life on October 1, 1972.

To date, the teachings of Neville Goddard are used as a source of inspiration and hope for many people across the world.

---

221 FREE Neville Goddard Lectures [930]

Correct Prayer (as described by Neville Goddard) [931]

---

[930] http://freeneville.com/221-free-neville-goddard-lectures/
[931] www.nirvikalpa.com/CorrectPrayer.doc

Freedom: Neville Goddard Simplified (an amazing $7) [932]
Book 3

Imagine: Neville Goddard Simplified (an amazing $7) [933]
Book 1

Imagination Creates Reality [934]

Mastering Self [935]

Mind Is Life (Neville Goddard videos) [936] [937]

Neville [938]

---

[932] http://freeneville.com/freedom-neville-goddard-simplified-volume-3/
[933] http://freeneville.com/neville-goddard-simplified-essential-keys-to-mastering-neville-goddard/
[934] http://www.mypowerlines.com/wp-content/uploads/2012/11/IMAGINATION-CREATES-REALITY.pdf
[935] https://archive.org/details/MasteringSelf
[936] http://www.mindislife.com/tag/neville-goddard
[937] http://www.youtube.com/user/mindislife?feature=watch
[938] http://www.i-am.cc/Neville/Neville.htm

Modeling Neville Goddard, Part 1 [939]

Modeling Neville Goddard, Part 2 [940]

Neville Goddard (Internet Archive) [941]

Neville Goddard Book Club (Facebook Page) [942]

Neville Goddard Coffee Club Videos [943]

Neville Goddard Daily Lessons [944]

Neville Goddard Forum: The Strangest Secret Is Within Your Imagination [945]

---

[939] http://nlplive.com/success-power-points/modeling-neville-goddard-part-1/
[940] http://nlplive.com/articles/modeling-tim-ferris-and-neville-goddard-part-2/
[941] http://archive.org/search.php?query=neville%20goddard
[942] https://www.facebook.com/nevillegoddardbookclub
[943] http://freeneville.com/coffee-club-videos/
[944] http://freeneville.com/category/neville_goddard_pdf/
[945]

http://profileengine.com/groups/profile/424718935/neville-goddard-forum-the-strangest-secret-is-within-your-imagination

Neville Goddard Lectures (Audio) [946]

Neville Goddard Lectures (Written) [947]

Neville Goddard Mastermind Group (Google) [948]

Neville Goddard MP3 (amazing cost of $27 US) [949]

Neville Goddard: The I AM [950]

Neville Goddard: Where to Begin? [951]

Neville Lessons [952]

Neville Notes [953]

---

[946] http://www.signsfromspirit.com/downloads-neville
[947] http://nevillegoddard.wwwhubs.com/Neville_Index.htm
[948] https://groups.google.com/forum/#!forum/neville-goddard-mastermind
[949] http://nevillegoddardaudio.com/neville-goddard-audio-collection/
[950] http://theiamblog.wordpress.com/tag/neville-goddard/
[951] http://freeneville.com/where-to-begin-with-neville-goddard/
[952] http://newthoughtthinkers.com/neville-goddard/neville-lessons-pdfs/
[953] http://nevillenotes.wordpress.com/

Power Explained: Neville Goddard Simplified (an amazing $7) [954] Book 2

Powerful Intentions: The Law of Attraction Community [955]

Revision: The Teaching of Neville Goddard [956]

Spiritual Psychotherapy [957]

The Core Teachings of Neville Goddard [958]

The Creative Use of Imagination [959]

The Intention Experiment Community [960]

---

[954] http://freeneville.com/power-by-neville-goddard-and-mr-twenty-twenty/

[955] http://www.powerfulintentions.org/forum/topics/neville-goddard

[956] http://www.blogtalkradio.com/illuminated-one/2013/12/19/revision-the-teachings-of-neville-goddard

[957] http://www.myspiritualpsychotherapy.com/neville.html

[958] http://freeneville.com/free-neville-goddard-pdf-the-core-teachings-of-neville-goddard/

[959] http://trueacu.com/The_Creative_Use_Of_Imagination

[960] http://community.theintentionexperiment.com/index.php?do

The Master Key to Wisdom [961]

=/group/neville-goddard/video/neville-goddard-the-world-
is-a-stage/
[961] http://masterkeywisdom.com/

Message 31

HEALING AND FORGIVENESS

Ho'oponopono (ho-o-pono-pono) is an ancient Hawaiian practice for reconciliation and forgiveness that provides a way to release the energy of painful thoughts, thereafter creating increased health, abundance and peace in your life.

Originally used in family situations where there was disharmony among family members, a mediator would be invited and Ho'oponopono would be used to make things right between them.

Ho'oponopono means *to make right*.

Ho'oponopono teaches that we are all created in the exact image of the Divine, but when our subconscious mind is full of negative memories (anger, resentment, blame) we lose this experience.

According to Ho'oponopono, the only way to be truly free and at peace with ourselves, no matter what is going on around us, is to receive inspiration from the Divine; this becomes possible when the memories in our subconscious mind are erased and transmuted to Zero (void) so that we can enjoy the experiences of being Divinity personified.

In 1976, Morrnah Simeona began to modify the traditional Hawaiian forgiveness and reconciliation process of Ho'oponopono to include the realities of the modern day, calling this Self-Identity through Ho'oponopono. [962]

This is an extremely simple strategy that, in its most basic form, involves you "cleaning" yourself by repeating, four simple phrases (silently, if you wish):

I'm sorry, Please forgive me, Thank you, I love you.

---

[962] http://being-free.com/images/stories/docs/The%20Twelve%20steps%20of%20Hooponopono%20PDF.pdf

While this may seem rather simplistic, the results can often be profound and life changing when people master the art of Ho'oponopono.

Robert F. Ray, author of <u>Return to Zeropoint II: Ho'oponopono for a Better Reality</u>, and a very dear friend of mine, offers workshops and seminars in how to utilize the principles of Ho'oponopono for emotional healing.

Ancient Hawaiian Ho'oponopono App [963]

Ho'oponopono Insights (Saul Maraney) [964]

The History of Ho'oponopono [965]

The Ho'oponopono River [966]

---

[963] http://hooponopono.wrhmedia.com/
[964] http://hooponoponoinsights.wordpress.com/
[965] http://soultransync.com/history-of-hooponopono/
[966] http://hooponoponoriver.com/

In reflecting back on Message 30, entitled The Intention Experiment, the waters of the Earth can be healed, as demonstrated through the research of Dr. Masaru Emoto. [967]

While it is clear to me that thought, emotions and music have an effect on water crystals, and the patterns that are formed, I invite you to draw your own conclusions.

Digital Biology and the Memory Effect of Water [968] [969]

DNA and Water Memory [970]

DNA Sequence Reconstituted from Water Memory? [971]

---

[967] http://www.masaru-emoto.net/english/water-crystal.html
[968] http://www.spiritofmaat.com/archive/dec3/bveniste.htm
[969] http://humansarefree.com/2011/04/water-has-memory-scientific-proof-from.html
[970] http://dnadecipher.com/index.php/ddj/article/view/8
[971] http://www.i-sis.org.uk/DNA_sequence_reconstituted_from_Water_Memory.php

Double-Blind Test of the Effects of Distant Intention on Water Crystal Formation [972] [973]

Effects of Distant Intention on Water Crystal Formation: A Triple-Blind Replication [974]

"Informationability" of Water and Origin of Life and Living Matter [975]

Memory of Water [976]

New Approach Controlling Cancer: Water Memory [977]

972
http://download.journals.elsevierhealth.com/pdfs/journals/1550-8307/PIIS1550830706003272.pdf

[973] http://noetic.org/library/publication-scholarly-papers/double-blind-test-effects-distant-intention-water/

[974] http://www.deanradin.com/papers/emotoIIproof.pdf

975
http://www.medicalbiophysics.dir.bg/en/water_memory.html

[976] http://www.life-enthusiast.com/memory-of-water-a-1084.html

[977] http://www.omicsonline.com/open-access/2090-8369/2090-8369-1-104.pdf

New Research Supports the Theory that Water has Memory [978] [979]

Nobel-Prize Winner Supports Homeopathy's "Memory of Water" [980] [981]

Scientists Investigate Water Memory [982]

The Electromagnetic Memory of Water [983]

---

[978] http://themindunleashed.org/2013/07/new-research-supports-theory-that-water.html

[979] http://topdocumentaryfilms.com/water-great-mystery/

[980] http://www.omicsonline.com/open-access/2090-8369/2090-8369-1-104.pdf

[981] http://www.theaustralian.com.au/news/health-science/nobel-laureate-gives-homeopathy-a-boost/story-e6frg8y6-1225887772305

[982] http://www.abovetopsecret.com/forum/thread939426/pg1

[983] http://www.fontainemagnetique.com/en/researchers/13-jacques-benvendiste/26-jacques-benveniste-et-la-memoire-electromagnetique-de-leau

The Memory of Water: A Critical Analysis of the Science behind a Homeopathic Theory [984]

The Memory of Water: An Overview [985]

The Mystery of Water [986]

Water Crystal Replication Study [987]

Water Has Memory [988]

984

http://www.homeopathycanada.com/sites/default/files/research-papers/irp-sarah-hutchinson.pdf
[985] http://www.badscience.net/files/MW2.pdf
986

http://www.oasishd.ca/index.php?option=com_content&view=article&id=181:art-the-mystery-of-water&catid=23:catt&Itemid=3
[987] http://deanradin.blogspot.ca/2009/01/water-crystal-replication-study.html
[988] http://thestillmind.wordpress.com/2013/07/26/water-has-memory/

Message 32

OPTIMISM

2012: The Best Year Ever [989]

This article shows that, on the macro level, our world is getting better all the time, primarily because people are coming together to make a difference, thereby working toward the building of a brighter future.

---

10 Reasons for Hope and Optimism [990]

If you watch the news, or read the newspaper, it seems as if everything is falling apart, mainly because the world is filled with war, fear, greed, and hate.

---

[989] http://www.wanttoknow.info/inspiration/best_year

[990] http://www.wanttoknow.info/inspiration/hope_optimism_rea sons

While these are the very challenges we are faced with, there are also many amazing developments taking place that the media seldom reports, mainly because fear-mongering and sensationalism is what sells.

This article outlines the 10 most inspiring trends, thereby further highlighting that despite the challenges, there are many great reasons for hope and optimism.

Building a Brighter Future [991]

Together, we can, and will, build a brighter future. In order to give meaningful suggestions to further support this, however, we first need to speak candidly about what is happening in the world at present; this article does just that.

---

[991] http://www.wanttoknow.info/brighterfuture

Message 33

FREE WISDOM COURSES

[1] The <u>Hidden Knowledge Course</u> is designed for those who want to dive into the deep cover-ups and hidden manipulations going on behind the scenes in our world.

While this information-packed course inspires readers to make a difference and build a better world, it is totally unlike the other courses, in that the focus is largely on exploring, and exposing, all that is hidden and secret in our world. This eye-opening course presents only reliable material which can be verified using provided links to respected sources.

Those who complete the course will have a broad understanding of the role of the power elite and how their plans often adversely impact life for the majority of people in our world.

[2] For those who choose to focus largely on love and inspiration, every page of the heart-expanding <u>Inspiration Course</u> will touch, move, and inspire you to open up to more love and deeper connections in your life.

With all of the violence and sensationalism prevalent in the media, this course feels like a fresh mountain breeze; so, too, does it feel like one is drinking water, so rich and fulfilling, from a pure mountain stream.

Herein, you will be uplifted and transformed by seeing humanity at its very best.

In these lessons you will find some of the most inspiring essays, videos, quotes and empowering exercises available on the Internet.

---

[3] Are you ready to be the change you want to see in your life and in our world? If the answer is yes, the <u>Insight Course</u> was designed for you.

Have you ever felt that one of the main reasons you are here is to help transform our planet to a new way of living based on love and empowerment?

Do you recognize that there is a divine essence in every person, and that as beautiful manifestations of the divine, all people deserve our love and support to be the best they can be?

[4] If so, the Transformation Course may be the choice for you; a course that harmonizes the light and inspiring aspects of life with the more challenging shadow sides of existence, thereby creating a beautiful synthesis which transcends duality.

These free online courses bring together the best of the Internet to both inspire and educate you in a dynamic and powerful way.

The journey through these courses will enhance your awareness, providing you with the necessary tools that will enable you to build a better life and world.

Course lessons will deepen your insight and expand your horizons, empowering you to be the change you want to see in the world.

<hr>

Which Course to Take? [992]

Table of Contents and Lesson Links for Wisdom Courses [993]

---

[992] http://www.wisdomcourses.net/which_course_to_take
[993] http://www.wisdomcourses.net/course_contents_wc

The Triad Wave

Brenda Williams was diagnosed with aggressive cancer in 1990; the first partial treatment created such intense side-effects, that the treatment was stopped.

Brenda never had another treatment; she went home with the understanding that she would die. One day, while she was sitting on her porch, she simply allowed herself to watch the wind in the trees; so, too did she take stock of the movement of the birds, the animals and the clouds in the sky.

Brenda became aware of subtle patterns of movement; as well, numbered sequences began coming into her mind, over and over again, until she finally took the sequence to a recording engineer.

As the engineer became involved in creating the sequence in audio format, they saw a wave on the computer screen; even though they were unable to *hear* the sequence, they were able to *feel* it.

Every individual seated in the waiting room, outside the soundproof studio, could also *feel* the sequence.

Not only did this 'silent wave' bring about Brenda's complete recovery from terminal cancer, it has also served to assist countless others.

Listen to Brenda Williams discuss the Triad Wave with Heather Macauley Noëll [994]

You can reach Brenda at <u>The Earth Project 777</u> [995]

The Triad Wave [996] [997]

Twin Flames Production [998]

---

[994] http://feelbetter.heathernoell.com/?page_id=9

[995] http://earthproject777.com/

[996] http://www.mindpowermp3.com/The-Triad-Wave/

[997] http://thefeelbetterprogram.com/experience-the-triad-wave/

[998] http://www.twinflamesproduction.com/TriadWave

Lucidity

Tim Freke, the founder of the Alliance for Lucid Living (ALL), a worldwide alliance of individuals who share a passion for the experience of lucid living, has been my foray into the world of Lucidity.

By way of definition, lucid living is ……

[1] a natural state of awareness that spontaneously arises when we wake up from the collective coma we mistake for 'real life' and appreciate the mystery of existence [999]

In continuation, lucid living is ……

[2] a state of super-clarity in which it becomes obvious that, although we appear to be separate individuals, in reality we are one awareness which is dreaming itself to be everyone and everything [1000]

---

[999] http://www.timothyfrekekc.com/lucidliving.php
[1000] Ibid.

So, too, is lucid living ......

[3] a beautiful experience of communion and compassion into which we dissolve when we see through the illusion of separateness and realize that all is one [1001]

I so appreciate what Tim shares in his book, How Long Is Now? A Journey to Enlightenment and Beyond: "I want to find a way to take people to the state I am experiencing myself, in which I'm *both* conscious that all is one *and* in love with the story of separateness." [1002]

In essence, we are all individuated aspects of the One, here to experience ourselves in all ways (hence, the individual stories), so that we can come to accept, appreciate and love both. Now, *that*, my friends, is awesome.

[1001] http://www.timothyfrekekc.com/lucidliving.php
[1002] Freke, Tim. (2009) How Long Is Now? A Journey to Enlightenment and Beyond (page 70). Carlsbad, CA: Hay House, Inc.

Consciousness and Spiritual Awakening (Tim Freke) [1003]

❖

LUCID DREAMS

How to Lucid Dream [1004]

Induce Lucid Dreaming Subliminal [1005]

Lucid Dreaming FAQ [1006]

Lucid Dreaming Techniques [1007]

The Lucid Dream Site [1008]

[1003] http://www.lifeartsmedia.com/tim-freke-consciousness-and-spiritual-awakening

[1004] http://www.wikihow.com/Lucid-Dream

[1005] http://www.realsubliminal.com/product/induce-lucid-dreaming

[1006] http://www.lucidity.com/LucidDreamingFAQ2.html

[1007] http://www.livinghealthy360.com/index.php/lucid-dreaming-techniques-to-improve-dream-consciousness-3-15553/

[1008] http://theluciddreamsite.com/lucid-living.html

The Lucidity Institute [1009]

LUCID LIVING

All Day Awareness [1010]

Experience Lucid Living (Craig Webb) [1011]

Lucid Living [1012]

Lucid Living: A Joyous, Sacred Journey [1013]

Lucid Living: A Mindful Moment [1014]

[1009] http://www.lucidity.com/
[1010] http://www.dreamviews.com/induction-techniques/113253-all-day-awareness-dild-tutorial-kingyoshi.html
[1011] http://craigwebb.ca/1-lucid_living.htm#
[1012]
http://www.kellysullivanwalden.com/30daydreamchallenge-day31/
[1013] http://www.lucidliving.net/
[1014] http://www.lucid-living.org/

Nothing Exists Unless You Are Aware Of It: The Power of Lucid Living and Nonduality [1015]

Real Magic Studies [1016]

LUCID LIVING (Tim Freke)

Entering the Mystery: A Key Step in Spiritual Awakening [1017]

Lucid Living in a Winter Wonderland [1018]

Lucid Living Meditation [1019]

[1015] http://www.enlightenmentpodcast.com/nothing-exists-unless-you-are-aware-of-it-the-power-of-lucid-living-nonduality/

[1016] http://www.realmagicstudies.com/RealMagicCourse/Hermetica.html

[1017] http://wisewaystohappiness.com/entering-the-mystery-a-key-step-in-spiritual-awakening/

[1018] http://wisewaystohappiness.com/lucid-living-in-a-winter-wonderland/

[1019] http://www.stillnessspeaks.com/ssblog/tim-freke-lucid-living-meditation/

The Mystery Experience [1020]

The Obsurd Notion of One [1021]

Tim Freke's Rapid and Direct Path to Awakening from Separateness [1022]

[1020] http://www.themysteryexperience.com/
[1021] http://soulbiographies.com/the-absurd-notion-of-one/
[1022] http://wisewaystohappiness.com/tim-freke%e2%80%99s-rapid-and-direct-path-to-awakening-from-separateness/

Being a Living Master

There is a secret place, a holy place, a precious place, a pure and uncontaminated place, that can be found in each and everyone.

It is a place of energy, a place of wisdom, a place of alchemy, that "will help us open our hearts, have more compassion, unconditional love, and empathy. It will strip away any of our differences and bring unity; but it will also trigger a new science . . . alchemy . . . of life." [1023]

An Ascended Master is one who, having obtained mastery and ascension before leaving this physical reality, works from higher realms to help humanity.

A Living Master is one who lives from mastery within a physical body.

[1023] http://www.alunajoy.com/2013-oct8.html

As you can see, being a Living Master is very different from being an Ascended Master.

When we start walking, and living, as Living Masters, it will also bring peace and harmony back to the world; this is something that we have been trying to do for a long time.
1024

It was Yeshua who stated … *What I have done, you can do also and greater things.*

The Earth is already transforming; how do we go about joining her in this process?

[1] Continue to maintain a humble heart.

[2] Keep love anchored in your heart.

[3] Treat everyone you meet with respect.

[4] Continue to honor yourself by following the power, love and wisdom that resides within your heart.

1024 http://www.alunajoy.com/2013-oct8.html

[5] Trust the process.

[6] Know that you are here to awaken to the consciousness of the *real* Self.

[7] Continue to move forward with a gentle strength and inner knowing that you are here to change the frequency of the planet.

[8] Know that you are here to anchor the power, the power of the Great Mother, the true power, the true strength of love, upon the planet.

[9] Know that you will be required to stand in your impeccability, your truth, your integrity, your responsibility, your veracity, your trustworthiness, no matter who you are (or who you think you are).

[10] Learn to walk, and work, in the place of centeredness in the heart without losing your focus, without losing your purpose, without losing your passion.

In keeping with John Lennon's *brotherhood of man*, we are an evolution in the making; the very evolution that he was able to foresee.

It has become clear that we are now living during the no time as so long ago prophesied by the ancients, a time of interface between worlds.

Embrace your inner wisdom.

Embrace the knowingness that these ancient texts spoke of us when writing the words *you who walk between the worlds,* for we were the ones standing on the precipice of a brand new world.

Since May 2012, Uranus in Aries has been square (90°) Pluto in Capricorn; at the most recent Winter Solstice 2013, Jupiter moved into opposition with Pluto, and in January 2014 Jupiter also squared Uranus, creating a T-square triangle. On April 12th, just three days before the Lunar Eclipse, Mars also moved into this pattern, opposing Uranus and completing the Grand Cross. [1025]

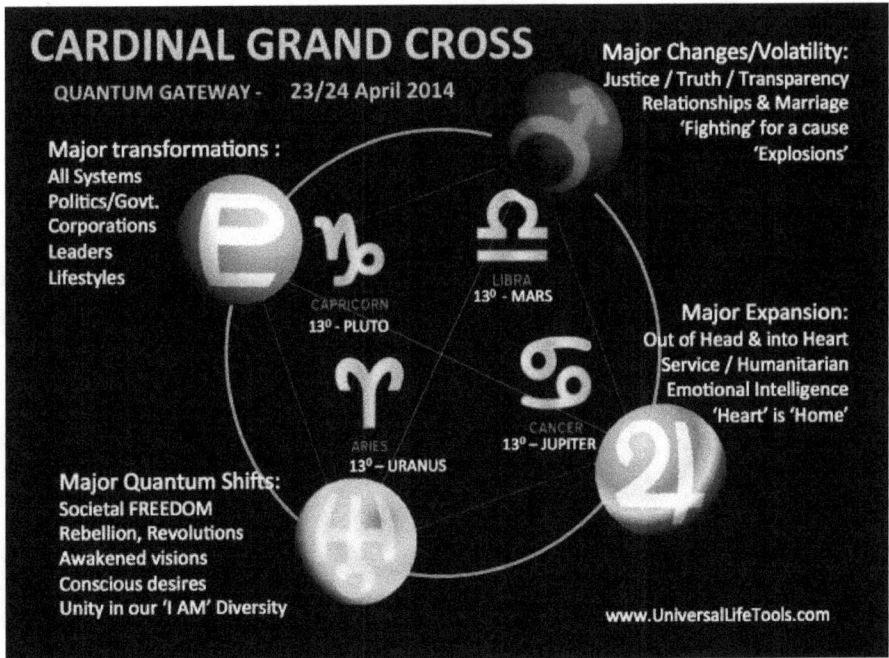

CARDINAL GRAND CROSS

QUANTUM GATEWAY - 23/24 April 2014

Major Changes/Volatility:
Justice / Truth / Transparency
Relationships & Marriage
'Fighting' for a cause
'Explosions'

Major transformations :
All Systems
Politics/Govt.
Corporations
Leaders
Lifestyles

CAPRICORN
13° - PLUTO

LIBRA
13° - MARS

Major Expansion:
Out of Head & into Heart
Service / Humanitarian
Emotional Intelligence
'Heart' is 'Home'

ARIES
13° – URANUS

CANCER
13° - JUPITER

Major Quantum Shifts:
Societal FREEDOM
Rebellion, Revolutions
Awakened visions
Conscious desires
Unity in our 'I AM' Diversity

www.UniversalLifeTools.com

1025

http://www.heavenandearthcommunity.co.uk/Blog.asp?PB MInit=1

From an astrological standpoint, the Uranus Pluto square has been the motivating energy behind the many revolutionary changes that have been taking place since 2012; as a result, more and more people across the globe are finding new ways to re-empower themselves, challenging long entrenched attitudes, to break through the lies and deceptions, in order to create a more honest and democratic world. [1026]

With Jupiter having entered in the fray, we are able to see the potential for a real and coherent vision for the future; it is imperative that we work towards creating new and positive goals, rather than just breaking down the old, without any clear vision of where we are heading. [1027]

With Jupiter situated in Cancer, everything is about creating a vision based on principles of care, compassion and nurture

---

1026

http://www.heavenandearthcommunity.co.uk/Blog.asp?PBMInit=1

[1027] Ibid.

for our family of fellow human beings; the exact opposite of power-based greed and manipulation. [1028]

When a Lunar Eclipse occurs after a Solar Eclipse, then it is more concerned with how we integrate the qualities brought by the Solar Eclipse; not so in this instance.

When a Lunar Eclipse precedes a Solar Eclipse, it requires a letting go to make space for us to receive the positive qualities that will be brought by the Solar Eclipse; which is currently the case.

Lunar Eclipse Grand Cross (April 15th)

As we challenge the 'accepted' or 'traditional' ways of doing things, we must use our intuition to see through the hidden or shady dealings of self and others; we are being guided to trust what we know in our hearts so that we can create new situations, based on right relationship. [1029]

[1028]

http://www.heavenandearthcommunity.co.uk/Blog.asp?PBMInit=1
[1029] Ibid.

Solar Eclipse Kite and Grand Cross (April 29th)

The Kite pattern, created by the Sun and Moon, during the time of the Eclipse brings with it the opportunity to heal the mistakes of our past, individually as well as collectively, by formulating our new vision and beginning to act upon it. [1030]

The Eclipse itself enables us to begin to reap the rewards that will be found by letting go of past attachments to wrong action, wrong thinking and wrong relationships; for it is in letting go of the past that we can move into a new future. [1031]

Now is the time for us to see, acknowledge, forgive and release.

This Eclipse offers us a clear and obvious choice. [1032]

[1] We can remain caught up with materialistic concerns.

1030

http://www.heavenandearthcommunity.co.uk/Blog.asp?PBMInit=1

[1031] Ibid.

[1032] Ibid.

We can continue to identify with the global dramas that are playing out on a daily basis, which merely continues to foster the illusion that we are all separate physical beings, with little real power to influence the world.

[2] We can step out of that illusion.

We can reclaim our spiritual power; in so doing, we can create a world based on compassion, wisdom and the knowledge that we are One with each other, the planet and all living beings.

With the planets in this configuration positioned in all four cardinal positions, these four signs (Aries, Cancer, Libra and Capricorn) are about initiating change.

If there are issues in your life that need your attention, now is the time to deal with them; denial is no longer an option. What can you do to overcome difficult situations that you have simply accepted for too long?

There is a Hopi prophecy that tells us the river is now flowing very fast; understandably, some people are afraid; these are the individuals that will try to continue to hold onto the safety of the shoreline, yet will be torn away.

Now is the time to demonstrate bravery by letting go of the shore and pushing into the flowing water with complete trust.

Reclaiming our spiritual power, in this way, means that we can begin to celebrate, in a sacred and caring manner, for we are the ones that we have long been waiting for.

It was Mahatma Gandhi who shared that *if we could change ourselves, the tendencies in the world would also change.*

As an individual, I am here to change the world one person at a time, beginning first, and foremost, with myself.

Thank You

If I may reiterate the words of Kristen Howe ...... [1033]

Thank you, thank you, thank you!

For what?

For being YOU!

You bring SO much to the world...

You are completely unique...

You are a magical, infinite being...

So, thank you for being here.

Because of you, the world is better!

You are extraordinary!

[1033] http://www.lawofattractionkey.com/

309

Final Words

In the astute words of Jonathan Swift ... *May you live all the days of your life.*

So, too, did he offer these fine words ... *Vision is the art of seeing things invisible.*

As well, he also wrote ... *No man was ever so completely skilled in the conduct of life, as not to receive new information from age and experience.*

If you think you know everything, great insights and wonderful new paths for exploration will simply pass you by.

Whilst much can be gleaned from books and blogs, the most important thing is *to live* and *to learn* from your experience(s), because it is there that you will continue to find the truest understanding of that which you seek.

I trust that this volume has served to guide you in the respect of getting to *know thyself.*

Until next time we meet – live well, be well, do well. [1034]

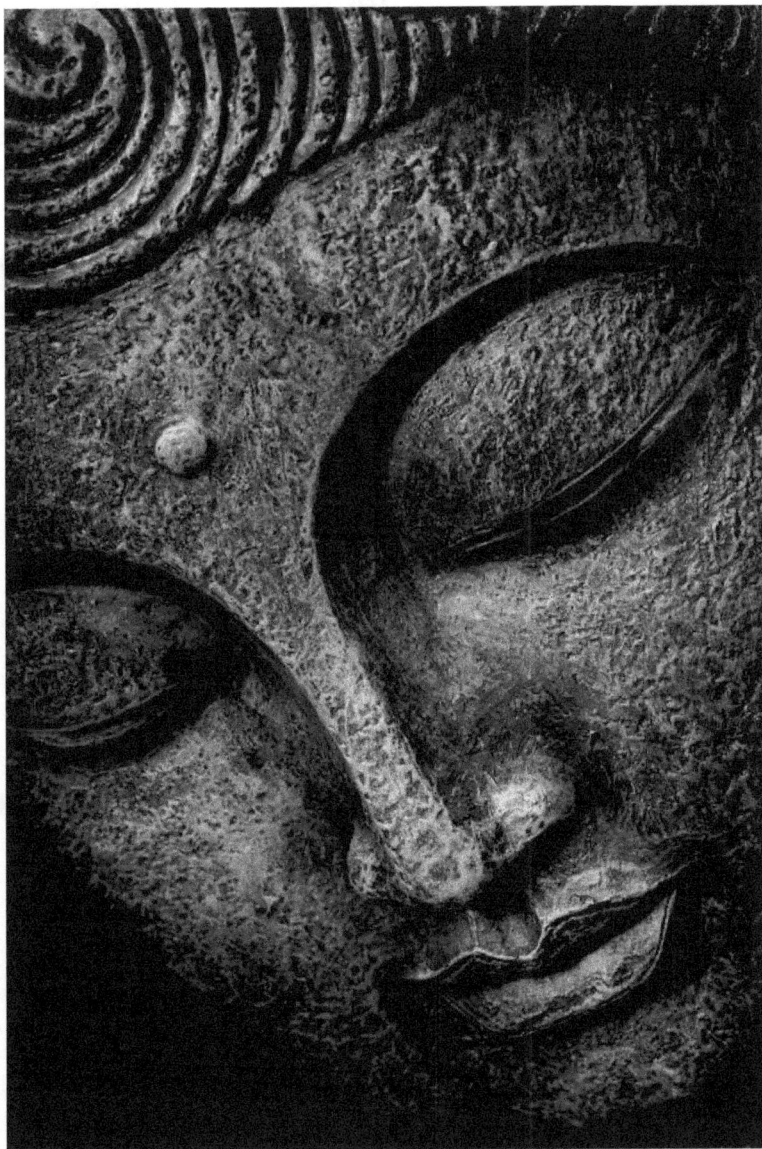

Bibliography

This bibliography is a collection of awesome websites. In addition, so, too, have I scoured the internet for sensational freebies, hoping that you, the reader, will enjoy all that is detailed herein.

ALTERNATIVE NEWS

AlterNet [1035]

Alternative News Links [1036]

Dissident Voice [1037]

The Utopian [1038]

[1035] http://www.alternet.org/
[1036] http://www.alternativenews.net/
[1037] http://dissidentvoice.org/
[1038] http://www.theutopian.net/

Truthout [1039]

Want To Know Info [1040]

WikiLeaks [1041]

Worldchanging [1042]

BLOGS

Earthcalm: The Ultimate EMF Protection [1043]

Steve Pavlina: Personal Development for Smart People [1044]

BUDDHISM

A Buddhist Library [1045]

[1039] http://www.truth-out.org/
[1040] http://www.wanttoknow.info/
[1041] http://wikileaks.org/
[1042] http://worldchanging.com/
[1043] http://www.earthcalm.com/emf-health/
[1044] http://www.stevepavlina.com/
[1045] http://www.abuddhistlibrary.com/

CHAKRA INFORMATION

Chakras (Claudia McNeely) [1046]

First Chakra video [1047]

COURSES

The Happiness Hop e-course (Tim Pond) [1048]

The Law of Emergence e-course (Derek Rydall) [1049]

CREATIVE VISUALIZATION

Creative Visualization Book List [1050]

Four Steps to Practical Creative Visualization [1051]

[1046] http://askclaudia.com/pdf/Chakras1.pdf

[1047] http://firstchakra.com/

[1048] http://tim-pond.com/free-happiness-hop-email-course.html

[1049] http://derekrydall.com/main/

[1050] http://www.portalsofspirit.com/books-creative-visualization/

[1051] http://www.clear-mind-meditation-techniques.com/support-

Visualization Book and Audio: Magical Imagineering Theater (Garin Bader) [1052]

DAILY READINGS

Angel Card Readings [1053] [1054] [1055]

Artistic State of Being Oracle Cards [1056]

Card of the Day Reading [1057] [1058] [1059] [1060]

---

files/creativevisualizationguidebook.pdf
[1052] http://www.coreforceenergy.com/free-visualization-book-and-audio-how-to-visualize/
[1053] http://www.angelmessenger.net/free-angel-card-readings/
[1054]

http://www.naturesworkshop.co.uk/AngelWingsCardReadin g.aspx
[1055]

http://signsofangels.com/Free_Online_Angel_Card_Reading .html
[1056] http://connectiontocreative.com/oracle-cards/
[1057] http://www.gregorygoldston.com/cardoftheday.htm
[1058] http://www.dianacooper.com/inspiration/pick-your-cards-for-today/
[1059] http://www.aquarianinsight.com/free-card-of-the-day-tarot-reading/

Crystal Spirits Reading [1061]

Gaian Tarot Reading [1062]

Goddess of the Moment Reading [1063]

Goddess Realm Four Card Spread [1064]

Inner Oracle Cards [1065]

Interactive Fairy Cards [1066]

Lightworker Cards [1067]

Self Healing and Guidance Notes [1068]

[1060] http://www.angelpaths.com/day.html

[1061] http://gitamaday.com/card-readings/crystal-spirits

[1062] http://www.gaiantarot.com/online-tarot-reading/

[1063] http://www.goddessrealm.com/goddess-of-the-moment

[1064] http://www.goddessrealm.com/four-goddess-card-spread

[1065] http://www.essentialpathways.com/free-oracle-card-readings

[1066] http://angelic-gifts.weebly.com/free-fairy-cards.html

[1067] http://www.lightworker.com/inspire/cards.php

[1068] http://www.divinegoddesshealing.com/free-guidance.html

FINANCIAL ABUNDANCE

Awakened Wealth Video Training 1 (Derek Rydall) [1069]

Awakened Wealth Video Training 2 (Derek Rydall) [1070]

Awakened Wealth Video Training 3 (Derek Rydall) [1071]

Awakened Wealth Video Training 4 (Derek Rydall) [1072]

Financial Abundance Dream Programming Audio [1073]

Guided Money Meditation [1074]

Million Dollar Experiment (Steve Pavlina) [1075]

[1069] http://derekrydall.com/aw-video/aw-video-1/video1.html
[1070] http://derekrydall.com/aw-video/aw-video-2/video2.html
[1071] http://derekrydall.com/aw-video/aw-video-3/video3.html
[1072] http://derekrydall.com/aw-video/aw-video-4/video4.html
[1073] http://freedreamprogrammingaudio.com/
[1074] http://guidedmoneymeditation.com/
[1075] http://www.stevepavlina.com/million-dollar-experiment.htm

Reconnecting With the Spirit of Money [1076]

GODDESS SPIRITUALITY

Books on Goddess Spirituality [1077]

INSPIRATION

Inspire 21 [1078]

Keys to The Ultimate Freedom: Thoughts and Talks on Personal Transformation (Lester Levenson) [1079]

[1076] http://ascension101.com/en/reconnecting-with-the-spirit-of-money.html

[1077] http://www.portalsofspirit.com/books-goddess-spirituality/

[1078] http://www.inspire21.com/

[1079]

http://www.stillnessspeaks.com/sitehtml/llevenson/keystoultimate.pdf

MANIFESTING

Future Visioning Manifestation Technique (Matt Clarkson) [1080]

Good Vibe University [1081]

Learn Manifesting: How to Manifest and Apply The Law of Attraction [1082]

Manifest Mastermind Blog [1083]

Manifesting Secrets [1084]

[1080]

http://www.mindbodymeditationsformanifesting.com/video/1.htm

[1081] http://www.goodvibeuniversity.com/public/main.cfm

[1082] http://www.learnmanifesting.com/

[1083] http://manifestmastermindblog.com/

[1084] http://mymanifestingsecrets.com/

Natural Hypnosis: Plant the Seeds of Natural Manifestation Package (contains three hypnosis sessions; namely Law of Attraction, Improve Visualization and Attitude of Gratitude) [1085]

Oprah's "O Dream Board" Vision Board Software [1086]

Project Yourself Reality Bending Course [1087]

Ten Years In The Future Exercise [1088]

MEDITATION

Books on Meditation [1089]

Gratitude Meditation [1090]

[1085] http://www.naturalhypnosis.com/package/seeds-of-natural-manifestation
[1086] http://www.oprah.com/spirit/O-Dream-Board-Envision-Your-Best-LifeTM
[1087] http://projectyourself.com/
[1088] http://tenyearsinthefuture.com/
[1089] http://www.portalsofspirit.com/books-meditation/
[1090] http://freegratitudemeditation.com/

Hack Your Mind: 7 Free Transformational Audios [1091]

Inner Guide Meditation [1092]

Meditation Room [1093]

Meditation Timer [1094]

MIND POWER

Books on Positive Thinking [1095]

Mind Power [1096]

Mind Your Reality: The Ultimate Resource for Mind Power and Conscious Reality Direction [1097]

[1091] http://mindvalleyacademy.com/featured/free-meditation

[1092] http://freeinnerguidemeditation.com/

[1093] http://www.freemeditations.co.uk/product-category/freemeditations/

[1094] http://freemeditationtimer.com/

[1095] http://www.portalsofspirit.com/books-positive-thinking/

[1096]

http://www.mindpowermp3.com/static_page.php?pageid=24
7

[1097] http://www.mind-your-reality.com/

Negative Emotions List [1098]

Pathways to Healing the Subconscious Mind [1099]

Positive Emotions List [1100]

Reprogramming our Subconscious, Part 1 [1101]

Reprogramming our Subconscious, Part 2 [1102]

Success Consciousness (Remez Sasson) [1103]

Success Manual Download Library [1104]

[1098] http://negativeemotionslist.com/

[1099] http://www.essentialpathways.com/guided-imagery-scripts

[1100] http://positiveemotionslist.com/

[1101]

http://www.chabad.org/kabbalah/article_cdo/aid/1914959/jewish/Re-Programming-our-Subconscious-Part-1.htm

[1102]

http://www.chabad.org/kabbalah/article_cdo/aid/1914971/jewish/Re-Programming-our-Subconscious-Part-2.htm

[1103] http://www.successconsciousness.com/free_ebooks.htm

[1104] http://www.successmanual.com/category/success-manual-downloads/

MUSIC

Spirit Tunes [1105]

Write Spirit Music Downloads [1106]

MOVIES

Sunrise Production Studio (link to three free movies) [1107]

Thrive [1108] [1109] is an unconventional documentary that lifts the veil on what is REALLY going on in our world by following the money upstream, uncovering the global consolidation of power in nearly every aspect of our lives. Weaving together breakthroughs in science, consciousness and activism, Thrive offers real solutions, empowering us with unprecedented and bold strategies for reclaiming our lives and our future.

[1105] http://www.spirittunes.com/

[1106] http://www.writespirit.net/resources/free-spiritual-music-downloads/

[1107] http://www.sunrise-production.org/

[1108] http://www.thrivemovement.com/the_movie

[1109] http://topdocumentaryfilms.com/thrive-what-on-earth-will-it-take/

NOETIC SCIENCES

Institute of Noetic Sciences (IONS) [1110]

Study Guide: What The Bleep Do We Know? [1111]

RESEARCH

Institute of HeartMath (free downloads) [1112]

The Energetic Heart: Bioelectromagnetic Interactions Within and Between People (HeartMath Institute) [1113]

SPIRITUAL MATERIAL (Audio files, Books, Reports)

Above Life's Turmoil audio (James Allen) [1114]

[1110] http://noetic.org/

[1111]

http://media.noetic.org/uploads/files/Bleep_Study_Guide.pd f

[1112] http://www.heartmath.org/free-services/downloads/free-download-library.html

[1113] ttp://www.metaphysics-for-life.com/support-files/energetic-heart_heartmathglobalcoherence.pdf

[1114] http://abovelifesturmoilaudio.com/

Acres of Diamonds audio (Russell H. Conwell) [1115]

As A Man Thinketh (James Allen) [1116]

Attaining Your Desires (Genevieve Behrend) [1117]

Awakening To Our Greatness (Rick Moss) [1118]

Daily Meditations (James Allen) [1119]

Dynamic Thought (Henry Thomas Hamblin) [1120]

Foundation Stones of Happiness and Success (James Allen) [1121]

Go Beyond The Secret [1122]

[1115] http://acresofdiamondsaudio.com/
[1116] http://asamanthinkethsoishe.com/
[1117] http://attainingyourdesiresfree.com/
[1118] http://www.essentialpathways.com/free-spiritual-ebook
[1119] http://jamesallendailymeditations.com/
[1120] http://henrythomashamblindynamicthought.com/
[1121] http://jamesallenfoundationstones.com/
[1122] http://icangobeyondthesecret.com/

Going Deeper: How To Make Sense of Your Life When Life Makes No Sense (Jean-Claude Koven) [1123]

How The Mind Works (Christian Larson) [1124]

How to Live Life and Love It (Genevieve Behrend) [1125]

In Tune With The Infinite (Ralph Waldo Trine) [1126]

Make a Ripple: Make a Difference (Camillo Løken) [1127]

Mastery of Fate (Christian Larson) [1128]

Memory Culture (William Walker Atkinson) [1129]

[1123]

http://www.prismhouse.com/sample.php?ID=prismhouse&IN=N

[1124] http://christianlarsonhowthemindworks.com/

[1125] http://howtolivelifeandloveit.com/

[1126] http://intunewiththeinfiniteralphwaldotrine.com/

[1127] http://www.one-mind-one-energy.com/make-a-ripple.html

[1128] http://christianlarsonmasteryoffate.com/

[1129] http://memoryculture.com/

Mental Efficiency audio (Arnold Bennett) [1130]

Mind Power: The Secret of Manifesting (William Walker Atkinson) [1131]

Mind Your Mind (Remez Sasson) [1132]

New Thought Library Authors [1133]

New Thought Library: Thomas Troward books [1134]

Obooko: Mind and Body Spirituality [1135]

[1130] http://mentalefficiencyarnoldbennett.com/
[1131] http://williamwalkeratkinsonmindpower.com/
[1132]

http://www.successconsciousness.com/free_ebooks/mind-your-mind.pdf
[1133] http://newthoughtlibrary.com/authors.htm
[1134]

http://newthoughtlibrary.com/trowardThomas/bio_troward.htm
[1135]

http://www.obooko.com/obooko_mind/free_ebooks_mind_body_spirit_001.html

Prosperity: How To Attract It (Orison Swett Marden) [1136]

PSI Tek Free Books (one of my all-time favorite sites) [1137]

Sacred Blueprints (Jazz Rasool) [1138]

Sadhana: The Realization of Life [1139]

The Christ Mind (Robert A. Clark) [1140]

The Eight Pillars of Prosperity (James Allen) [1141]

The Game of Life audio (Florence Scovel Shinn) [1142]

The God Principle (John Rekesh) [1143]

[1136] http://orisonswettmardenprosperity.com/
[1137] http://www.psitek.net/index2.html#gsc.tab=0
[1138] http://www.energydiamond.com/sacredblueprints/
[1139] https://librivox.org/sadhana-by-rabindranath-tagore/
[1140] http://www.thechristmind.org/thechristmind.pdf
[1141] http://eightpillarsofprosperity.com/
[1142] http://thegameoflifeaudio.com/
[1143]

http://books.google.ca/books?id=FKm2kooCSNgC&printse
c=frontcover&redir_esc=y#v=onepage&q&f=false

The Greatest Thing Ever Known (Ralph Waldo Trine) [1144]

The Greatest Thing In The World audio (Henry Drummond) [1145]

The Heavenly Life audio (James Allen) [1146] [1147]

The Idea Made Real (Christian Larson) [1148]

The Kybalion (The Three Initiates) [1149] [1150]

The Law and The Word (Thomas Troward) [1151]

The Life Triumphant (James Allen) [1152]

[1144] http://thegreatestthingeverknown.com/
[1145] http://greatestthingintheworld.com/
[1146] http://theheavenlylifeaudio.com/
[1147] https://librivox.org/the-heavenly-life-by-james-allen/
[1148] http://christianlarsontheidealmadereal.com/
[1149] http://kybalionpdf.com/
1150

http://www.yourdivineinheritance.com/Books/The_Kybalion.pdf
[1151] ttp://www.successmanual.com/free-success-ebook-law-and-the-word-thomas-troward/
[1152] http://jamesallenthelifetriumphant.com/

The Magic Story (Frederick Van Rensselaer Day) [1153]

The Master Key System (Charles F. Haanel) [1154] [1155]

The Master Mind (Theron Q. Dumont) [1156]

The Mastery of Destiny (James Allen) [1157] [1158]

The Miracle of Right Thought (Orison Swett Marden) [1159]

The Napoleon Hill Success Library [1160]

The Path to Prosperity (James Allen) [1161] [1162]

The Power of Concentration (Theron Q. Dumont) [1163]

[1153] http://themagicstorypdf.com/
[1154] http://freemasterkeysystemcharlesfhaanel.com/
[1155] http://www.one-mind-one-energy.com/ebooks.html
[1156] http://theronqdumontmastermind.com/
[1157] http://jamesallenmasteryofdestiny.com/
[1158] http://masteryofdestinyaudio.com/
[1159] http://orisonswettmardenrightthought.com/
[1160] http://www.successmanual.com/category/napoleon-hill-success-library/
[1161] http://pathtoprosperitynow.com/
[1162] http://pathofprosperityaudio.com/
[1163] http://theronqdumontpowerofconcentration.com/

The Prophet (Kahlil Gibran) [1164]

The Science of Being Great (Wallace Wattles) [1165] [1166]

The Science of Being Well audio (Wallace Wattles) [1167]

The Science of Getting Rich (Wallace Wattles) [1168] [1169] [1170] [1171]

The Shift of the Ages: Convergence Volume 1 (David Wilcock) [1172]

[1164] ttp://www.metaphysicalteachers.com/category/bios-of-metaphysical-teachers/
[1165] http://scienceofbeinggreatfreedownload.com/
[1166] http://thescienceofbeinggreataudio.com/
[1167] http://scienceofbeingwellaudio.com/
[1168] http://scienceofgettingrichfreedownload.com/
[1169] http://www.one-mind-one-energy.com/ebooks.html
[1170] http://freescienceofgettingrichaudio.com/
[1171] http://thescienceofgettingrichvideo.com/
[1172] http://divinecosmos.com/start-here/books-free-online/18-the-shift-of-the-ages

The Science of Oneness: Convergence Volume 2 (David Wilcock) [1173]

The Divine Cosmos: Convergence Volume 3 (David Wilcock) [1174]

The Strangest Secret video (Earl Nightingale) [1175]

The Way of Peace (James Allen) [1176]

Think and Grow Rich (Napoleon Hill) [1177]

Think and Grow Rich, Part 1 [1178]

[1173] http://divinecosmos.com/start-here/books-free-online/19-the-science-of-oneness
[1174] http://divinecosmos.com/start-here/books-free-online/20-the-divine-cosmos
[1175] http://play.simpletruths.com/movie/the-strangest-secret/
[1176] http://thewayofpeacejamesallen.com/
[1177] http://www.one-mind-one-energy.com/ebooks.html
[1178]

http://mymillionairemind.org/motivation_selfimprovement/think-and-grow-rich-part-one/

Think and Grow Rich, Part 2 [1179]

Think and Grow Rich, Part 3 [1180]

<u>Thoughts Are Things</u> (Prentice Mulford) [1181]

<u>Thought Vibration</u> audio (William Walker Atkinson) [1182]

<u>Your Forces and How to Use Them</u> (Christian Larson) [1183]

<u>Your Invisible Power</u> (Genevieve Behrend) [1184]

[1179]

http://mymillionairemind.org/motivation_selfimprovement/think-and-grow-rich-part-two-creative-visualization-and-taking-action/

[1180]

http://mymillionairemind.org/motivation_selfimprovement/think-and-grow-rich-%e2%80%94-part-three-%e2%80%94take-action/

[1181] http://prenticemulfordthoughtsarethings.com/

[1182] http://thoughtvibrationaudio.com/

[1183] http://christianlarsonyourforcesandhowtousethem.com/

[1184] http://getyourinvisiblepower.com/

SUBLIMINALS

Real Subliminal (Deep Calm) [1185]

UNIVERSAL TRUTHS

20 Universal Laws [1186]

A Conscious Creation Overview (Seth and Jane Roberts) [1187]

A Cosmic Symphony [1188]

Advaita Vedanta and Quantum Physics: How Human Consciousness Creates Reality [1189]

[1185] http://www.realsubliminal.com/free-subliminal-mp3

[1186] http://www.one-mind-one-energy.com/20-universal-laws.html

[1187]

http://www.paulhelfrich.com/library/Helfrich_P_Seth_Jane_Roberts_Conscious_Creation_Overview.pdf

[1188] http://maris-greenriver.com/

[1189]

https://www.dccc.edu/sites/default/files/faculty/francesco_bellini/advaita-vedanta-and-quantum-physics-aar-presentation.pdf

Aeon Magazine [1190]

A Handbook for Lightworkers [1191]

Aligning Energy [1192]

A Journey to Oneness: A Chronicle of Spiritual Emergence (Rasha) [1193]

Articles on Personal and Planetary Transformation [1194]

Bashar (channeled information) [1195]

Bashar: Receiving The Reality You Desire [1196]

[1190] http://aeon.co/magazine/
[1191] http://affinityseries.com/lightworker/
[1192] http://www.kjmaclean.com/AligningEnergy.html
[1193]
http://www.amazon.com/exec/obidos/ASIN/0965900347/portalsofspirit
[1194] http://www.alunajoy.com/articles.html
[1195] http://www.bashar.org/
[1196]
http://api.ning.com/files/nbvq1gS8ah0jsxqAgMskwEcuoFz BCfRkut05jvLLqL6W-

Books on World Transformation and Selfless Service [1197]

Changing The Paradigm of The Planet (Jeddah Mali) [1198]

Conscious Creation [1199]

Conscious Creation (Myke Wolfe) [1200]

Conscious Creation Journal Archives [1201]

Conscious Creation Radio Show [1202]

Conscious Creation Tips (Jackie Lapin) [1203]

VTizQ-vuNKPwCFcPHcn*y95tcfJwuwesSL8kElb*cRTvCZplZ-i1/BasharReceivingtheRealityYouDesire.pdf

[1197] http://www.portalsofspirit.com/books-world-transformation-and-selfless-service/

[1198] http://www.jeddahmali.com/about.php

[1199] http://www.consciouscreation.com/

[1200] http://www.consciouscreation.info/lawofattraction/manifesting/creating_reality.php

[1201] http://www.consciouscreation.com/journal/

[1202] http://www.blogtalkradio.com/consciouscreation

[1203] http://consciouscreationtips.com/

Consciousness and the Conscious Universe [1204]

Consciousness Shifts Reality (Cynthia Sue Larson) [1205]

Creative Manifesting (Anisa Aven) [1206]

Divine Cosmos (my favorite website) [1207]

Evolution Ezine Free Gifts [1208]

Golden Age of Gaia [1209]

Hermes Trismegistus (Tom DeLiso) [1210]

Higher Balance Institute (Eric Pépin) [1211]

[1204] http://www.bibliotecapleyades.net/ciencia/ciencia_conscious universe.htm
[1205] http://www.realityshifters.com/
[1206] http://www.creatavision.com/creative-manifesting.htm
[1207] http://divinecosmos.com/
[1208] http://evolutionezine.com/category/free-gifts/
[1209] http://goldenageofgaia.com/
[1210] http://www.wisdomsdoor.com/index1.htm
[1211] http://www.higherbalance.com/

How Consciousness Creates Reality [1212]

How To Create A Reality That Exceeds Your Dreams [1213]

How to Create Your Reality With the Power of Your Imagination [1214]

How We Create Reality [1215]

Jeshua Channelings (Pamela Kribbe) [1216]

Life Of Learning Foundation Self-Realization School (Guy Finley) [1217]

Lightsmith (Michele Mayama) [1218]

[1212] http://free-will.de/reality.pdf
[1213] ttp://www.oakcreekprintworks.com/core/wp-content/uploads/2010/09/A-B-C-of-Success.pdf
[1214] http://www.drdilip.com/articles/imagination.pdf
[1215] http://www.wakingtimes.com/2013/04/06/how-we-create-reality/
[1216] http://www.jeshua.net/
[1217] http://www.guyfinley.org/
[1218] http://www.lightsmith.com/

Mind Your Reality (Tania Kotsos) [1219]

Morphogenetic Resonance: From Causal to Conscious Creation (Lauren C. Gorgo) [1220]

Notes From The Universe [1221]

Oneness (Rasha) [1222]

Personality and Spirit: Discovering Who and What We Are [1223]

Planet Lightworker Magazine [1224]

[1219] http://www.mind-your-reality.com/
[1220] http://spiritlibrary.com/lauren-c-gorgo/morphogenetic-resonance-from-causal-to-conscious-creation
[1221] http://www.tut.com/inspiration/
[1222] http://www.amazon.com/exec/obidos/ASIN/0965900312/portalsofspirit
[1223] http://personalityspirituality.net/
[1224] http://www.planetlightworker.com/

Ramtha: A Beginner's Guide to Creating Reality [1225]

Reality Creation 1010 [1226]

Soulful Living [1227]

Spirit of Now (Peter Russell) [1228]

Spiritual Dynamics Academy [1229]

Spiritual Science Research Foundation [1230]

The Abundance Site [1231]

[1225] http://103.9.88.89/app/2014-01-11/Ramtha%20-%20A%20Beginners%20Guide%20to%20Creating%20Reality.pdf

[1226] http://www.redshift.com/~beyond/real1010.html

[1227] http://www.soulfulliving.com/

[1228] http://www.peterrussell.com/index2.php

[1229] http://www.spiritualdynamics.net/

[1230] http://www.spiritualresearchfoundation.org/

[1231] http://www.theabundancesite.com/

The Adventure of I: A Journey to the Centre of Your Reality (Tania Kotsos) [1232]

The Aquarius Paradigm [1233]

The Art of Conscious Creation (Jackie Lapin) [1234]

The Art of Conscious Creation (Tom Murasso) [1235]

The Big Picture (one of my favorite websites) [1236]

The Conscious Creation of a New Paradigm [1237]

The Consciousness Chronicles [1238]

The Elias Forum [1239]

[1232] http://www.amazon.com/exec/obidos/ASIN/0957677006/portalsofspirit

[1233] http://aquariusparadigm.com/

[1234] http://jackielapin.com/the-art-of-conscious-creation/

[1235] http://borntomanifest.com/articles/tom5.html

[1236] http://www.kjmaclean.com/

[1237] http://www.spiritofmaat.com/archive/mar2/tiller1.htm

[1238] http://conscious-pictures.com/chronicles/cc_index.html

[1239] http://www.eliasforum.org/

The Great Wealth Pandemic (Jody Sachse) [1240]

The Higher Consciousness Forum [1241]

The Kryon Handbook [1242]

The Law of One (Ra material) [1243] [1244]

The New Enlightenment [1245]

The Physical World as a Virtual Reality [1246]

The Quantum Matrix (Adrian P. Cooper) [1247]

[1240] http://freepdfs.org/pdf/the-great-wealth-pandemic
[1241] http://higherconsciousnessforum.com/free-spiritual-ebooks/
[1242] http://www.kryon.com/k_25b.html
[1243] http://www.lawofone.info/
[1244]
http://www.llresearch.org/library/the_law_of_one_pdf/the_law_of_one_pdf.aspx
[1245] http://www.hermes-press.com/
[1246] http://arxiv.org/ftp/arxiv/papers/0801/0801.0337.pdf
[1247]
http://www.ourultimatereality.com/newsletters/TheQuantumMatrix.pdf

The Tenets of Seth [1248]

The Universe is Mental: Secrets of Mind and Reality [1249]

Enoch Tan is a mind and reality scientist and writer who uses the internet as the medium with which to help people achieve higher awareness in living and experiencing life. He wants to impact the world in the biggest way possible by changing lives and creating possibilities.

Educational psychology states that a learned person is one with a vision of unified knowledge.

In turn, Enoch does not like being restricted to seeing things from one dimension, preferring to see things from multiple dimensions in order to combine them into an integrated perspective.

[1248]

http://www.gestaltreality.com/downloads/Summary,%20Ten ets,%20Quotes%20of%20the%20Seth%20Material.pdf
[1249] http://www.mindreality.com/mindreality.pdf

If any of these words resonate with you, please take the time to support his work. You can also get a taste for the type of material he writes in keeping with his archived articles. [1250]

The Words of Oneness (Rasha) [1251]

Time 2 Wake Up: 20 Keys Of Conscious Creation [1252]

Trans4Mind Personal Development Resources [1253]

Universal Principles [1254]

Welcome to the Divine Science Online [1255]

Wisdom Teachings with David Wilcock [1256]

[1250] http://www.mindreality.com/archive

[1251] http://www.onenesswebsite.com/

[1252]

http://www.newciv.org/nl/newslog.php/_v397/__show_articl e/_a000397-000252.htm

[1253] http://www.trans4mind.com/index3.html

[1254] http://www.arnoldpatent.com/wordpress/universal-principles/

[1255] http://thedivinescience.org/

[1256] http://www.gaiamtv.com/show/wisdom-teachings-david-wilcock

Wisp Magazine (a Reality Creation magazine) [1257]

Wizard's Wonderland [1258]

Words of Wisdom [1259]

When Consciousness Changes the Physical World [1260]

Who is the "You" in You Create Your Own Reality? [1261]

YOGA

Sun Salutation: The Perfect Yoga Workout [1262]

[1257] http://wisp.focusphere.net/

[1258] http://www.wizardwonderland.com/

[1259] http://www.trans4mind.com/quotes/quotes-spiritual.html

[1260] http://realityshifters.com/media/RealityShiftsBookExcerpt.pdf

[1261] http://www.paulhelfrich.com/library/Helfrich_P_Who_is_the_You_in_YCYR.pdf

[1262] http://www.artofliving.org/sun-salutation

Affiliate Links

To be an affiliate means to be an agent for that product.

Simply put, when you enroll as an affiliate, you promote (or sell) the product of the site (or company) you are enrolled with. You are given an affiliate link wherein you use that link for promotion of the product. When someone clicks on your affiliate link and buys the product you are promoting, you earn a commission for the product sold.

As an affiliate, I believe in sponsoring the products that I have personally tested. Given my spiritual journey of the past 20+ years, there have been a great many products (as you are about to see) that have served, and are continuing to serve, me well.

Your support in purchasing through these links enables me to empower more people worldwide to live more conscious lives and for that I take the time to thank you.

Four Categories of Brain Wave Patterns

Beta (14-30 Hz)
Concentration, arousal, alertness, cognition

Higher levels associated with anxiety, unease, feelings of separation, fight or flight

Alpha (8-13.9 Hz)
Relaxation, super-learning, relaxed focus, light trance, increased serontonin production

Pre-sleep, pre-waking drowsiness, meditation, beginning of access to unconscious mind

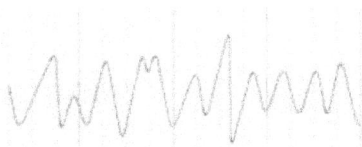

Theta (4-7.9 Hz)
Dreaming sleep (REM sleep)
Increased production of catecholamines (vital for learning and memory), increased creativity

Integrative, emotional experiences, potential change in behavior, increased retention of learned material

Deep meditation, access to unconscious mind

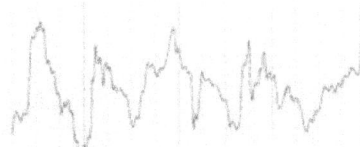

Delta (0.1-3.9 Hz)
Dreamless sleep
Human growth hormone released

Deep, trance-like, non-physical state, loss of body awareness

Access to unconscious and "collective unconscious" mind, greatest "push" to the brain

http://www.behappy101.com/images/categories-of-brain-waves.jpg

BRAINWAVE ENTRAINMENT

▶BRAIN SALON (Karl Moore) [1263]

The Brain Salon is a scientifically-proven MP3 series that uses specialized sound patterns to change your state of mind.

[1263] http://www.brainsalon.com/demo/?a=Chebogue

347

Each of the six audio sessions are designed to bring about a specific state of mind. Just slip on your headphones and get ready for instant results.

▶BRAINWAVE EVOLUTION SYSTEM (Karl Moore) [1264]

The Brain Evolution System (or BrainEv, for short) is a powerful, scientifically-proven 6-level brainwave MP3 program that uses specially created sounds to influence your brainwaves, safely shifting you into a deep state of peak performance, on-demand!

Developed through BrainEv Labs, led by brainwave entrainment pioneer Michael Kelley, the program launch was supported by an investment of over $500,000.

Since then, the Brain Evolution System has become respected as one of the most life-changing programs on the market today.

[1264] http://www.brainev.com/demo/?a=Chebogue

The Brain Evolution System can help you release stress and tension, sharpen your thinking skills, help you feel happier, rocket your IQ, increase your energy levels and master your emotions ... all you have to do is listen to one of the brainwave MP3s, for 30 minutes a day.

Sound interesting? Take the time to join us.

►GENIUS BRAIN POWER (Cameron Day) [1265]

Science has proven that *the human brain is the most complex and powerful computing machine we have ever seen*, but are we really using all that computing power?

The *traditional methods of upgrading your brain* for super-human levels of genius *involve hours of daily meditation* and other disciplines designed to force the brain to adapt to extreme circumstances. Fortunately, science and modern technology have developed a way, courtesy of brainwave entrainment, to impart the peak brain states experienced by seasoned meditators, Buddhist monks, Yogis and top level athletes.

[1265] http://b62351w3jinpolf7mrg2cyho26.hop.clickbank.net/

Utilizing computer generated, rhythmically pulsed beats (known as Isochronic beats), *Genius Brain Power* safely, gently and effectively guides your brain to entrain you to your most optimal brainwave frequencies.

►INFINITE BRAIN POWER SYSTEM (Todd Lee) [1266]

A program unlike any success program you have ever heard of because it works for you on 100% pure auto-pilot!

All you need to do is plug into and listen to our scientifically engineered sessions and let them get to work on re-wiring your brainwaves for success.

Based on a solid foundation of research and development and actual proven and tested results over the last 75 years; founded on work deserving of a Nobel Prize, the information found in the program is totally revolutionary in every way.

[1266] http://8318e0r2plpjnl9dq0p9pdr5rz.hop.clickbank.net/

▶NITROFOCUS (Karl Moore) [1267]

Discover the scientific solution to increasing your productivity.

Nitrofocus is a simple MP3 audio program, designed to increase your productivity, by activating your "focus brainwaves." It works by mixing special brainwave tones, which get your brain into The Zone, with distraction-blocking background sounds.

The result? A simple collection of MP3s (backed by science) that you can listen to while you work, each helping you increase focus and get more done in less time.

▶SLEEP SALON (Karl Moore) [1268]

The Sleep Salon is a brainwave audio program that works by using special tones and pulses, which help influence your brainwave patterns.

[1267] http://www.nitrofocus.com/gift/?a=Chebogue
[1268] http://www.sleepsalon.com/?a=Chebogue

Listening to this audio gently takes you down from a waking Alpha state into a deep Delta sleep.

Incredibly powerful and totally safe, the Sleep Salon merely improves on what the brain does naturally, lulling you into a deep sleep within minutes.

Just hit the Play button and listen as you fall asleep. No headphones are required, and you will probably never hear the end of the recording.

The Sleep Salon contains 12 brainwave MP3 sessions. Just read the user guide and listen to the one most suited to the type of insomnia that you are experiencing.

► SONIC VITAMINS [1269]

Welcome to Sonic Vitamins, the Web's leading supplier of MP3 brainwave sessions, for significantly changing your mood.

[1269] http://www.sonicvitamins.com/sonic/?ref=48106

Just slip on your headphones, listen to an MP3 "shot" and watch it change how you feel.

From deep relaxation to faster thinking, increased energy to deep sleep, these scientifically-proven recordings use computer-generated sounds to influence the brainwaves, altering how you feel, in just 30 minutes.

Which Sonic Vitamin pill would you like to take today?

▶THE MORRY METHOD ™ [1270]

A Brainwave Entrainment expert, Morry worked with the Brazilian Government to train officers to reach their peak performance. [1271]

All Morry Method™ recordings are mixed to ensure a harmonic balance of sound, science and technology (a combination that provides the maximum effects possible; so, too, do they also follow a strict adherence to comprehensive scientific research.

[1270] http://www.themorrymethod.com/
[1271] http://www.themorrymethod.com/TMMResearch-FIN.3.pdf

[1] QUANTUM CONFIDENCE (Morry Zelcovitch) [1272]

When it comes to manifestation, making, and maintaining, the change from a negative state (frustrations, worries, doubts, fears, anxieties) to a positive state (total self confidence, high self esteem) is of utmost importance because until you change the way you think, you will simply continue to manifest more of the same (which is usually what you do not want).

In creating the *Quantum Confidence* system, Morry Zelcovitch has created a responsible, scientific and considerate way to help people identify and deal with what may be holding them back.

Using the *Quantum Confidence* system is very similar to sticking to an exercise regimen or even a proper diet that includes a change in eating habits. Once you get to the point where you want to be, it is important that you keep up a maintenance routine in order to maintain your achieved results.

[1272] http://c6719bqacevsot5cyw0hx9sbp6.hop.clickbank.net/

The affirmations are designed for each hemisphere of the brain.

So, too, are they designed to be accepted by your mind so that change, real change, may occur in the most efficient and effective way possible.

For those of you who have never used this system (which involves brainwave entrainment), there is something that you should be made aware of.

Brainwave entrainment, when properly engineered, has been shown to allow for the release of deep trauma that has been buried.

Please consider having someone nearby (a professional, a trusted friend, a family member) with whom you can discuss these issues as they arise.

In many cases, repressed emotions and events clear themselves easily, but occasionally they may be difficult.

As people are listening to TMM recording systems, they find that random thoughts continue to pop out of nowhere. Do not fight these thoughts. Simply allow them to be.

It is important to keep remembering that when you resist something, you are engaging in a state of stress.

This program is all about natural states of relaxation, peace and bliss.

[2] QUANTUM MIND POWER (Morry Zelcovitch) [1273]

The *Quantum Mind Power* (with TMM) system uses various "sculpted" tones and embedded frequencies in order to get the brain to go into altered (but very natural) states of consciousness.

When the brain reacts to these tones, beneficial neurotransmitters and endorphins are released (which are necessary neuro-chemicals that our brain and body need to function properly, healthfully and naturally).

[1273] http://cc73e7kzkamouzbh191ptf0te1.hop.clickbank.net/

When the brain is stimulated with pulses, the overall activity of the brain will respond to, and align with, these pulses. By selecting the desired rate, the brain, via the frequency following response (entrainment), can be naturally induced towards the selected brainwave state.

Neural Synergy was specifically designed to help to re-organize the brain to a higher level; allowing it to process more complicated stimuli easier than before.

An integral part of a fitness regimen for the brain, this recording should be listened to once a day.

Eden Energy Wave Dynamics is designed to pump up your energy levels, while silencing the "voices" that tend to make you stagnate and stop moving forward (because they make you think too much, or cause you to fear something).

This recording may be rotated with *Neural Synergy* on alternate days for variety and/or whenever you feel the need for a quick "pick me up."

Whole Brain Gratitude Meditation was designed as a gratitude building meditation. This recording, which is intended to be listened to twice a week, helps you with direction and intent, thereby enabling you to change your current view of the world (which then changes your reality as well). How you look at things and interpret their meaning can be everything, and amazing changes occur when you change how you look at life.

Emotive Brain Wave Hypnosis was designed to help guide you to balance your emotions and experience happiness, allowing you to tap into the deep wiring of your subconscious mind (so that you can better deal with the matters that are most affecting your life). It is intended to be listened to twice a week.

Feel free to sample a 20 minute audio recording. [1274]

[3] SPECIALLY PRICED FACEBOOK SPECIALS [1275]

[1274] http://quantum-mind-power-system.com/Gift-for-friends.htm

[1275] http://www.themorrymethod.com/tmm.php?id=20

► TRYPNAURAL BRAINWAVE ENTRAINMENT MEDITATION (Niraj Naik) [1276] [1277] [1278]

Niraj Naik (a musician and scientist with classical training in ancient Indian Vedic and Gregorian music) discovered a strange relationship between music, brainwaves and the harmonic pulse of our planet (the Schumann Resonance).

He recognized that music played with a hypnotic arpeggiated groove at 120bpm and 60bpm would sync perfectly with alpha and theta brainwaves and the Earth's magnetic pulse.

This discovery is what led to the development of this brand new style of brainwave entrainment; a breakthrough meditation technology designed to *stimulate your natural production of tryptamines* (serotonin, melatonin and DMT) so you can benefit from deeper sleep, improved mood, increased mind power, better health, creativity and intuition.

[1276] http://c6f251lzpkjslwb0s4-ynq3s5r.hop.clickbank.net
[1277] http://www.trypnauralmeditation.com/blog/
[1278] http://www.trypnauralmeditation.com/subliminal-healing/

As these Trypnaural products feature the beautiful music of amAya (a collaboration between Niraj Naik and Dr Mrigank Mishra, both with an expertise in crafting exquisite sounds and music with a healing touch), their sublime and unique style of music has been gaining incredible popularity, with their music being used in therapy centers, yoga studios and health spas all around the world. [1279]

You get access to a frequently updated library of Trypnaural meditation tracks, brainwave entrainment sessions, raw isochronic tones and nature sounds.

You also get special guides that teach you how to create your own subliminal mind programs and guided meditations using free tools that you can find online.

BREATHING

►THE POWER OF BREATHING [1280]

[1279] http://www.amayasounds.com/
[1280] http://www.powerofbreathing.com/?ref=48106

For millennia, cultures across the world have known about the magical power of breathing.

Not only does it sustain human life, but it can bring about huge benefits if used correctly.

Backed by years of scientific research, breathwork is one of the simplest, most powerful methods of changing your life (just by changing the way you perform this common human function).

This revolutionary breathwork audio course steadily guides you through a series of expertly-crafted breathing sessions, designed to stimulate the life-changing, healing benefits of breathwork.

Starting with the Level 1 session (8 minutes), you steadily progress to the more powerful breathing patterns in Level 2 (10 minutes), before ultimately advancing to Level 3 (15 minutes).

You will instantly enjoy a feeling of calmness and total mental clarity; many of the deeper benefits will be realized within a couple of weeks.

Enjoy the sessions in the morning, and/or in the evening, whenever you need a mental boost and wish to sharpen your mind.

CHAKRA WORK

▶ALIGNING TO ZERO SUBLIMINAL ALIGNMENT AUDIO [1281]

This is a 30 minute downloadable track that is not music; it is a vibrational drone that matches and cycles through your 7 different energy centers (chakras).

Experts agree that aligning our chakras awakens and enhances our consciousness to a higher state of awareness; so, too, do we experience increased relaxation, relief from stress, increased ESP talents, accelerated healing, enhanced imagery, creative breakthroughs, aligned hormones and an instant *in the flow* state.

Our energy centers are challenged on a daily basis; the number one cause of misalignment is stress.

[1281] http://5c21b-oaegpius4oy0s55q2kcz.hop.clickbank.net/

When your body is in alignment, it can heal itself in ways that modern medicine has been trying to do for hundreds of years.

New research indicates that sound and music both contribute, in a positive way, to our emotional and physical well-being.

Subliminal Alignment harmonically achieves these results in the same way that Tibetan monks have used bowls, bells and overtone chanting for centuries.

►CHAKRA 7 SYSTEM [1282]

This 22 hour training video course is designed to teach you how to reinvigorate and heal your 7 chakras. Carol Tuttle brings together a selection of key modern and traditional healing methods which give you the freedom to uplift and strengthen your chakras in a way that best suits you. Get ready to tap into your chakras and see improvements in every aspect of your life.

[1282] http://mval.li/?a=3010&c=331&p=r&s1=

CREATIVE VISUALIZATION

▶BEYOND MANIFESTATION (AN ADVANCED MANIFESTATION SYSTEM) [1283]

These audio recordings of the historic seminar go beyond The Attractor Factor, The Power of Intention, Ask and It Is Given, Beyond *Positive Thinking*, The Secret, and virtually every other "How to Manifest" or "Law of Attraction" book, course, or movie out there.

If you want more and are ready for more, you need look no further.

If you are ready to learn how to turbocharge your ability to manifest, this is it.

If you are ready to go beyond what you know or think you know, here is your chance.

If you are ready to let go of what doesn't work in order to learn (and embrace) that which does, you are there.

[1283] http://ee3d00m-dmjpgt28wvonhras17.hop.clickbank.net/

If you are open minded, get ready to brace yourself for some powerful goosebumps.

►MAKE YOUR VISUALIZATIONS A REALITY (Steve G. Jones) [1284]

To put it clearly and succinctly, if you have *not* created a clear and concise vision of how you will achieve financial independence within your mind, then what you have done is created a vision of how you will not achieve it.

In other words, by *not* using visualization to your advantage, you have used it to your disadvantage and perhaps created a vision of yourself working for someone else or just not making the money that you need to be financially free.

Aside from intense training and practice, professional athletes mentally visualize themselves achieving the desired result. This makes it much easier for them to do so in real life situations because the mind cannot tell the difference between an event experienced in real life and a created within the mind.

[1284] http://c04a7ys3g8rotva7-qrj9vnn6h.hop.clickbank.net/

This, alone, is what makes visualization such a powerful tool.

Clinical hypnotherapist, Steve G. Jones, has been helping people effectively master creative visualization, through the power of hypnosis, for over 25 years.

Taking everything he has learned and discovered, he has created a truly empowering program (that consists of four audio modules, approximately 30 minutes each) to help people master using visualization in the privacy of their own home.

▶ Refer back to the chapter entitled MIND MOVIES.

▶ QUANTUM JUMPING [1285]

Quantum Jumping is an advanced visualization exercise that will enable you to tap into your subconscious mind and discover an infinite number of realities and possibilities.

[1285] http://mval.li/?a=3010&c=463&p=r&s1=

After spending decades studying meditation, yoga, hypnosis and a variety of other spiritual and metaphysical disciplines, Burt Goldman invented Quantum Jumping in 2008.

Get ready to discover the shocking mind trick (used for centuries by some of the world's most prolific artists, inventors and entrepreneurs) that can help you master any skill, achieve any goal, and live a life of success and fulfillment.

► THE POWER OF CREATIVE VISUALIZATION WITH LISA NICHOLS [1286]

Creative Visualization is a collection of 12 guided meditation audios delivered by Lisa Nichols, based on elements from Shakti Gawain's Creative Visualization and the Silva Method.

Lisa's teachings will take people on an *experiential carpet ride* into their future from a very organic, practical and tangible place of touch, smell, feel and experience.

[1286] http://mval.li/?a=3010&c=961&p=r&s1=

HEALTH AND WELL-BEING

▶ THE FIVE RITUALS [1287]

Hidden deep inside the Himalayas is a secret *almost* too good to be true. It is a secret that can enable you to look a shocking 30 years younger.

It is a secret that can remove your wrinkles. It can restore your natural hair color. It can improve your memory. It can correct your eyesight. It can turbo-charge your energy levels, your strength and your virility.

While this is a strong claim, it is not made lightly.

These are the exact same Five Rituals that were passed onto Peter Kelder, who went on to write The Ancient Fountain of Youth and The Eye of Revelation whereby he documented the amazing power of these five rituals, and how they had the power to radically make anyone look and feel better.

[1287] http://www.fiverituals.com/?ref=48106

Kelder's work received critical acclaim when it was published in 1939. In just ten minutes a day, you will be seeing results within one week.

HYPNOSIS

▶PEAK PERFORMANCE HYPNOSIS (Niraj Naik) [1288]

Fall into a deep sleep in minutes and wake up to peak mental performance, everyday, using the ground breaking Trypnosis Audio Technology, the core of this unique transformational system.

Tell them where to send your free Conscious Mind Trpnosis Primer session (designed to prime your mind for positive change). [1289]

LAW OF ATTRACTION

▶ATTRACT STUDIO [1290]

[1288] http://f779e6j4e8tnfsfjyd3z0o9y2w.hop.clickbank.net/
[1289] http://peakpowerhypnosis.com/
[1290] http://www.attractstudio.com/?ref=48106

The Law of Attraction works but most people don't get the results, because they are not visualizing the right way.

Visualization is the most important step in the manifestation process.

It focuses your thoughts, keeps your purpose on track, and sends out 'vibrations' that attract those desires into your life.

Many of us who do visualize actually shift our vision along the way by changing what we want.

Others do not add enough emotion to their visualization, leaving the "signal" they send out both limp and lifeless.

Many of us have major problems with the visualization process.

In other words, the vast majority of individuals get nowhere near the powerful results they expect from the Law of Attraction, simply because they are not visualizing the right way.

Why not take the time to create Attraction Movies?

Essentially, they are animated vision boards, incorporating all of your goals and desires.

They use images, videos, music and affirmations, to create an enticing movie, completely customized to your goals.

Attraction Movies are powerful, evoking a wave of; they also consistently highlight your specific goals, without any wavering or change along the way.

Attract Studio is a powerful collection of workbooks, video and audio, that takes you straight to being a Law of Attraction Pro.

► DECODING THE ABUNDANCE MINDSET [1291]

What are the driving forces that inspire people who excel in every field?

What makes them different, gives them that edge?

What are the secrets to their success?

[1291] http://38be0ak4onnfqt86tmwghc5c62.hop.clickbank.net/

Do you wonder why you see success all around you, but aren't experiencing it first-hand? It may be because you are unwittingly blocking your successes and sabotaging yourself with doubts, uncertainties, and limiting beliefs on a subconscious level. To create and attract what you want, your mind must first be convinced of your ability to succeed in all levels of awareness, both *consciously* and *subconsciously*.

This online, multi-media course is designed to help you [1] remove the invisible barriers to your success, [2] unlock your hidden creativity, [3] discover the laws of a successful life, [4] break the cycles of repeating patterns that don't get you what you want, and [5] assist you in manifesting and creating all that you do want.

►LAW OF ATTRACTION CERTIFICATION PROGRAM [1292]

[1292] http://3c4568m5ncnfhl99302dbf1o67.hop.clickbank.net/

►LAW OF ATTRACTION WEALTH PRACTITIONER CERTICATION PROGRAM [1293]

►LAW OF ATTRACTION PRO (Bradley Thompson) [1294] [1295]

You have tried *The Secret*. You have bought manifestation books. You may even have attended a seminar, but you are still *not* getting results with the Law of Attraction.

Bradley Thompson knows why.

In his latest audio course, Bradley distils wisdom from the world's leading Law of Attraction teachers, to bring you the ultimate guide to manifestation success.

►LIFE VISION MASTERY [1296]

To get going on a better way forward, one thing is for sure: you need to have a vision.

[1293] http://b904c9x2hesssq0htwo9461673.hop.clickbank.net/
[1294] http://www.lawofattractionpro.com/?ref=48106
[1295] http://www.lawofattractionpro.com/science.html
[1296] http://fl73fzp6iajsgk29yegq83vw0g.hop.clickbank.net/

Famous deaf and blind author, Helen Keller, once pointed out that *the most pathetic person in the world is someone who has sight, but has no vision.*

And Steven Covey, in his book <u>The 7 Habits of Highly Effective People</u>, has also recommended, *begin with the end in mind.*

Put simply, visioning is about how you would like things to be. It involves having the image of your desired end result as a reference by which you undertake physical actions towards manifesting it.

However, as you will find out later, it is not just any vision that you would want to adopt.

You would want to align with one that connects with your heart, through a higher awareness of who you are.

You also want to learn about how best you can work together with the laws of the Universe so that you can turn your ideal mental picture to reality more easily and effortlessly.

The *Life Vision Mastery Program* is a home-study course that guides you on a heart-centered journey, for the purpose of self-discovery, visioning and bringing your dreams forward.

It is a series of practical journaling-and-visualization exercises that culminates in your making of a vision board.

The *Life Vision Mastery Program* is one that offers you the tools to bring your best life forward.

▶THE ABSOLUTE SECRET (Bradley Thompson) [1297]

There is a single secret that connects a long-lost *Little Red Book* (published in 1926), the world famous software billionaire, Bill Gates, and one very special, well-known, Quantum Physics experiment.

When the student is ready, the teacher will appear.

[1297] http://www.theabsolutesecret.com/?ref=48106

If you are ready to open your life to success, happiness, joy, wisdom, friendships, unlimited wealth and freedom, this might be something that you want to explore.

▶THE BELIEF SECRET (Bradley Thompson) [1298]

In 1948, Claude Bristol published a book that unveiled the *real* secret behind manifestation; BELIEF.

Belief changes both yourself and the world around you. What you expect to happen, very often happens. With belief, your perceptions shift, the world around you changes, and opportunities can become more apparent.

Believe and you can really receive.

▶THE QUANTUM COOKBOOK [1299]

Having manifested a dream lifestyle over the past 20 years, Bradley Thompson knows the two missing steps that The Secret does not tell you.

[1298] http://www.beliefsecret.com/?ref=48106
[1299] http://www.quantumcookbook.com/?afl=48106

He will prove to you that manifesting works brilliantly when you follow his 6 step program. Not only that, but he will hand over $150 if it does not work for you. This just might be something that you also want to check out for yourself.

LIFE COACHING

►LIFE COACHING SECRETS (Bradley Thompson) [1300]

MANIFESTATION

►DELIBERATE CREATION INSTANT SELF-HYPNOSIS (Dr. Robert Anthony) [1301]

Your conscious mind is your everyday normal state of awareness.

Your subconscious mind is your connection with your Higher Intelligence.

[1300] http://www.life-coaching-secrets.com/?ref=48106

[1301] http://hop.clickbank.net/?chebogue/tsdc1129&x=6minaudio

Between your conscious and subconscious, there is a gatekeeper that Dr. Anthony calls the Critical Factor.

This Critical Factor takes what your conscious mind is thinking and seeks approval from the subconscious mind to pass the information along; sometimes it allows it to be delivered and sometimes it does not.

The subconscious operates on the principle of least effort, meaning that it likes things the way they are (routine) and hates change.

The function of this gatekeeper is to keep things the same; its primary intention is to make your life easier by rejecting information that does not match the Subconscious Blueprint you already have inside. In some cases, this proves quite useful (so that you do not do something stupid), but in other cases it can actually be harmful (keeping you stuck with a belief or a habit that you no longer want).

As well, this gatekeeper uses powerful tools (like fear, doubt, worry and anger) to automatically reject new information, meaning that it needs to be bypassed in order to replace hidden (subconscious) blocks and beliefs.

It is quite possible to *consciously* override what your subconscious mind has been programmed to do. Mind you, when your conscious mind gets distracted, your subconscious mind takes over again and you simply revert back to living the same as before.

Hypnosis bypasses the gatekeeper to give you unlimited, creative access to rewrite the Blueprint in your subconscious so that it finally gives you everything you want out of life without any effort or struggle.

By going to the place where the problem exists and resolving it, you create true freedom and the ability to live life on your terms.

Deliberate Creation Instant Self-Hypnosis sets up an artificial mechanism to trigger this process.

►EMERGINEERING PERSONAL DEVELOPMENT SYSTEM (Derek Rydall) [1302]

Whether you are an artist, entrepreneur, writer, teacher, coach, or healer, you can activate your emerging power in every area of your life and actualize more potential than you ever thought possible.

►ENLIGHTENED BEINGS SUPER MANIFESTOR E-STORE [1303]

An e-store that sells manifesting ebooks, affirmation ebooks, guided meditations and a manifesting e-course, all courtesy of Jafree Ozwald, an absolutely amazing Manifestation Coach.

►SOUL PURPOSE BLUEPRINT (Derek Rydall) [1304]

You have been taught the exact reverse of how life works.

[1302] http://www.1shoppingcart.com/app/?Clk=5137396
[1303] https://www.enlightenedbeings.com/SM-estore/index.php?r=1&ref=211
[1304] http://www.1shoppingcart.com/app/?Clk=5137402

Bombarded by messages from the moment you were born (you can't do this, you can't be this, what you want is impossible), as a coping mechanism to protect this precious core, you began to close off parts of your authentic, powerful, brilliant, gorgeously outrageous self.

Is it any wonder that you have continued to struggle to know who and what you are and the great purpose you were born for?

Even after becoming aware of what might be possible, is it any wonder why you have had a hard time accepting your potential and really going for it?

Re-connecting to your Soul Purpose Blueprint (that divine DNA) and *bringing your life back into alignment with it* will heal those lifelong traumas, and re-integrate those buried treasures, so that you will never be a victim of circumstances again.

▶THE LAW OF EMERGENCE (Derek Rydall) [1305]

[1305] http://www.1shoppingcart.com/app/?af=1559591

In Derek's words ... *Self-Improvement is an oxymoron. The Self, when truly understood, is already perfect. Just as the acorn contains the oak, the Self has everything it needs to fulfill its higher purpose. When the inner conditions are right, it naturally emerges; bigger, better, and more abundantly than we can imagine. This isn't hyperbole, it's law; the Law of Emergence. Practicing it will enable you to live on the emerging* edge, *where your greatest potential can unfold in every area of your personal and professional life.*

▶THE SECRET OF DELIBERATE CREATION (Dr. Robert Anthony) [1306]

This program is a dynamite combination of <u>The Da Vinci Code,</u> <u>The Secret</u> and <u>Think and Grow Rich</u>.

Mysterious, suspenseful, and powerfully persuasive, it is now available in a considerably discounted (of over $100) and fully downloadable version.

[1306] http://b514ayx6qnjkjq7n15h-dodod8.hop.clickbank.net/

What Dr. Robert Anthony does in *The Secret of Deliberate Creation* is show you how the natural laws of Quantum Physics, the Law of Attraction, and Cause and Effect can either work for you or against you.

As a conscious and deliberate creator, you, too, will want these laws working for you, 100% of the time.

MEDITATION

▶CORE ENERGY MEDITATION [1307]

Scientists have recently made some amazing discoveries about the human bio-energy field and the major energy centers in the body.

These energy centers literally determine how good (or bad) you feel each day.

The better you feel, the more you are able to attract the good things you want into your life.

[1307]

http://www.mindbodytrainingcompany.com/go.php?Clk=40 73087

Kevin Schoeninger (certified holistic fitness trainer, meditation instructor and Reiki Master/Trainer) has developed a 20-minute practice that will balance all your major energy centers.

This is a short daily practice that allows you to balance and energize every aspect of your being; a practice that better enables you to feel healthy and happy (which is all part of your life purpose).

Kevin's *Core Energy Meditation* system also gives you a blueprint for tapping into your personal guidance system. When you feel connected to Source, you know when you are taking the right action for your life in the here and now.

▶ENNORA BINAURAL BEATS [1308]

Ennora Binaural Beats are special meditation music recordings that entrain your brain for better health and well-being, helping to reduce stress and anxiety, increase

---

1308

http://dbbbdbicghmmft150bwmmocke4.hop.clickbank.net/

focus and productivity, improve sleep, heighten spiritual consciousness and more.

Simply listen through headphones and relax; it's that easy.

▶ OMHARMONICS [1309]

OmHarmonics is a revolutionary audio meditation product designed and developed after a year of devoted attention by Mindvalley and a team of world-class consciousness engineers.

Powered with binaural beats, heartbeat synchronization and ambient sounds, *OmHarmonics* stimulates your senses in a positive way and is scientifically proven to eliminate internal and external resistance to allow you to reach an optimal meditative zone in a matter of minutes.

[1309] http://mval.li/?a=3010&c=563&p=r&s1=

▶THE SECRETS OF MEDITATION, HEALTH AND MANIFESTATION [1310] is a comprehensive introduction to meditation, breathing, energy work and manifestation.

What many do not realize is that there are meditation and breathing exercises you can use to reduce stress as well as improve your health, thereby increasing your level of energy and enjoyment of life.

These secrets are simple and yet tremendously powerful. Doing these exercises on a daily basis, as simple as they are, will change your life.

These secrets include how to [1] develop control over your own mind and body, [2] supercharge your energy level and feel great on a day-to-day basis, and [3] work with the power of your subconscious mind to move you toward what would truly fulfill you in your life.

1310

http://www.mindbodytrainingcompany.com/go.php?Clk=40 73086

Matt Clarkson has created a complimentary course to help you get started. With each installment, you will get an exercise, inspirational message or tip, to help you calm the mind and reduce stress.

This is an ideal program for anyone with an interest in meditation, self-growth and personal development, as well as for anyone suffering from stress, anxiety or depression.

▶SPIRITED MEDITATION (Steve G. Jones) [1311]

The positive effects of spiritual mediation have been known for thousands of years.

People from all over the worlds have used spiritual mediation to attain a higher degree of enlightenment since the beginning of time.

Some people however, find it difficult to meditate.

[1311] http://56e464u8lnlspx8kyb1bzgqa8c.hop.clickbank.net/

With so many thoughts running wild within our minds, clearing the mind and achieving the state of pure consciousness can be quite a task.

Achieving the state of pure consciousness in spiritual mediation involves much of the same things that are involved in hypnosis.

The problem was that for many years, getting people to achieve the Alpha state was something that could only be done during a private session at outrageous cost.

Determined to find a better solution, world renowned hypnotist, Steve G. Jones, found a way to create a program that people could use to master the art of spiritual meditation and provide an overall benefit to their life wherever and whenever they wanted.

▶THE POWER OF PRACTICE [1312]

1312

http://www.mindbodytrainingcompany.com/go.php?Clk=40
73090

If you have had any kind of trouble making The Law of Attraction work in your life, you may be missing one key ingredient, as is shared by Mind-Body Training expert Kevin Schoeninger.

This is the program wherein you will discover the one word never mentioned in <u>The Secret</u>, a concept that is crucial for your happiness and success with the Law of Attraction.

Kevin calls this the Master Tool as used by Oprah, Donald Trump, and all of the great spiritual masters that live their soul's purpose, while also manifesting spectacular results.

► THE MEDITATION PROGRAM [1313]

Your brain operates at certain frequencies, depending on what it is doing.

When you are sleeping, you are experiencing Delta. Right now, as you are reading this text, you are in Beta. When you begin meditating, you start delving into lower Alpha.

[1313] http://www.meditationprogram.com/?ref=48106

After you have been meditating for years, you start to be able to reach newer, more powerful depths – levels of deep Alpha, deep Theta, and even upper Delta (the levels where you begin to experience profound benefits).

There *is* a way to achieve these depths without having to commit years of your life to daily meditation.

By using binaural beats, a technique discovered in 1839 by German research scientist, Heinrich Wilhelm Dove.

During the process of playing slightly different frequencies into the left and right ear, a third frequency (binaural beat) is generated; the brain automatically follows this frequency, putting you into that very state of mind.

This means that by listening to deep Alpha, deep Theta and upper Delta frequencies, you will be able to quickly replicate states of deep meditation.

Through the process of meditation, you expand the threshold of your mind, thereby giving it more "space" to operate, and automatically releasing negative self-sabotaging habits along the way.

This Meditation Program includes a series of levels, each designed to take you deeper and deeper, expanding the threshold of your mind, bringing you a greater sense of peace and understanding with each session.

Consisting of eight brilliantly-composed levels, each taking you deeper that the last, each level is designed to be listened to for at least a week, at which point you move onto the next.

Levels 1 to 4 begin expanding the threshold of your mind, gradually exploring the deepest states of Alpha.

Levels 5 to 7 cover deep Theta and early Delta.

Level 8 expands your mind into the mid-Delta stage. When you reach this frequency (of about 2.5 Hz), you will be experiencing the most powerful meditation available, something that typically takes years to achieve.

Rather than simply containing the sounds of rain, like most competing products, each level in *The Meditation Program* contains a unique, deep and powerful soundtrack compiled by industry-leading composer, M. Anton. [1314]

Meditation is changing; the Meditation Program is where you need to be.

MIND POWER

▶ SUPER MIND EVOLUTION SYSTEM [1315]

Since Einstein has proven that energy and mass are interchangeable, various universities and laboratories have been able to either measure or calculate the force generated by a human mind (as in psychokinetic experiments).

The obvious conclusion here is that, as mass and energy are interchangeable, the energy generated by human consciousness can be converted into its mass equivalent, the format of which is controlled and directed by the most

---

1314

http://cdn.selfdevelopment.net/meditationprogram.com/mp3/sample.mp3

1315

http://www.supermindevolutionsystem.com/store/?12737

extraordinary of higher-consciousness processes; namely, visualization.

When a human mind clearly, and continually, visualizes an end result, with deep emotion and concentrated intent, then the formatted energy generated is converted into its mass equivalent (meaning the desired result).

Jim Francis, a serious researcher, has a background in both hypnosis and electronic design. The founder of the Australasian Lateral Thinking Newsletter, he has been its editor for the past twelve years.

Having undertaken training in various forms of remote viewing, Jim shows how this medium technique can easily be learned.

Apart from Jim's description of his mind discoveries and their application, he also points to the serious science that supports his concepts, describing how individuals can take advantage of these scientific suppositions, thereby moving towards a better understanding of how the intuitive mind works.

The substantiated research of Jim Francis, over the course of the last 10 years, was combined with the latest *cutting edge* brain audio technology. As a result, the *Super Mind Evolution System* was born.

The entire system is available in 21 PDF reports and 20 audio mp3 files, all accessible via instant download.

▶REVOLUTIONIZ: HARNESS THE HIDDEN LAWS OF THE UNIVERSE [1316]

If you have struggled to understand *exactly* how the Law of Attraction brings abundance and prosperity into your life, all it requires is a relatively small shift in your understanding of how life works.

You may have read all the books on the subject and watched movies like *The Secret* and many others and *still* do not understand the fine intricacies of these universal mechanisms, much less how you can steer them.

[1316] http://0bc880v9fniijw0mwf56v8kk97.hop.clickbank.net/

In lacking full understanding (because you might be overwhelmed by the barrage of half-truths and myths that prevail), the way you are subconsciously interacting with the universe might actually be bringing you more of the very things you do not want.

Once you learn, once you realize and appreciate the power of understanding the Universal Principles of Life in the way you are about to learn them, courtesy of this program, you can and will draw all the love, money, success, health and happiness you have been longing for directly into your life.

► THE UNDISCOVERED PARALLEL, PART 1 [1317]

Discover *The Undiscovered Parallel Part 1* which will show you one simple trick to supercharge all techniques used for focusing your mind (as in visualization, affirmations, subliminals, hypnosis, EFT, the Sedona Method, meditation, brainwave entrainment, counseling or therapy) as part of your self-growth journey.

[1317]

http://www.mindbodytrainingcompany.com/go.php?Clk=40 85676

NLP (NEURO LINGUISTIC PROGRAMMING)

► THE ULTIMATE NLP COURSE [1318]

NLP (Neuro Linguistic Programming) was co-created by Dr. John Grinder and Dr. Richard Bandler.

Powerful and completely safe, NLP contains so much theory that most people never really get started; the books are too thick and the Advanced Master Practitioner courses can take *months* to complete.

Having crammed years of NLP training down to an awesome new two hour course, we want to show you the techniques that really work and produce amazing results.

For the first time ever, Certified NLP Practitioner Christine Golden has crystallized her years of NLP knowledge into the most dynamic NLP training course available today.

No waiting.

No confusion.

[1318] http://www.ultimatenlp.com/?ref=48106

No trying to decipher instructions from a guidebook.

Just sit back, listen, and witness the change for yourself.

► THE NLP SECRET [1319]

NLP one of the most powerful methods of changing your thoughts in the quickest time possible.

Often used as an alternative to psychotherapy, it works by talking to your brain in its own "language" and altering how you think about things.

To begin, you find a negative pattern that happens automatically in your life (or in the life of your client, if you are a therapist). Negative patterns include feelings such as shyness, fear, stress, procrastination, anger and feeling stuck.

Once you have identified the problem, you simply perform a little trick (that takes about 10 minutes) involving the body.

No years of therapy.

[1319] http://www.nlpsecret.com/?ref=48106

No weeks of training.

Are you ready to enjoy total change, and access the NLP Secret for yourself?

SPIRITUAL AWAKENING

▶BEYOND CONSCIOUSNESS (Steve G. Jones) [1320]

Beyond Consciousness: 8 Subconscious Techniques to Change Your Life is a new program that combines the power of hypnosis, lucid dreaming, meditation, astral projection, astral sex, the Third Eye, and even the Akashic Records to bring peace, clarity, balance and happiness back into any person's life.

To put it simply, if you are experiencing any kind of stress, negativity or imbalance right now, you can use this program to eliminate these negativities from your life so you can be happier and more satisfied with life.

[1320] http://b3d6b5p6knlisxelmhubvr3q9u.hop.clickbank.net/

If your problems have been weighing you down, now is the time to throw away those heavy boulders that you have been carrying and *fly* to the heights of the Akashic Records and astral realms.

Today marks the beginning of your new life, with this 8-part audio training, available for immediate download as mp3 audio files, and a PDF transcript of all 8 modules.

▶THE AWAKENING COURSE (Joe Vitale) [1321]

This Awakening Course will take you on a magical journey through the four stages of awakening. During your adventure, Joe will instruct you on the pitfalls and practices of each stage before finally leading you into the fourth and final stage of complete awakening; a place rarely described.

▶THE SOUL JOURNEY [1322]

[1321] http://cbe2aambnanltyf7bvodv-gl48.hop.clickbank.net/
[1322] http://www.thesouljourney.com/?a_aid=195

People everywhere are searching for well-being (meaning, purpose, fulfillment, health and happiness). For life to be good, we need to feel useful and appreciated.

Taking a spiritual growth journey called *The Soul Journey* will enable you to grasp the bigger picture of who you are. You will discover how to distinguish your personality from soul. You will learn practical ways to develop and express soul for a life of meaning and purpose.

In changing your consciousness, you will change your life.

SUBLIMINALS

▶CREATIVE VISUALIZATION WITH SUBLIMINAL SUGGESTIONS: POWER MIND SERIES (Nelson Berry) [1323]

▶MASTER MANIFESTER SUBLIMINAL MESSAGES VIDEO SERIES (Nelson Berry) [1324]

[1323] http://1e5355mzeappftal64rk-1bma0.hop.clickbank.net/
[1324] http://a65c73m-limmszfqw1nj55ey38.hop.clickbank.net/

►SUBLIMINAL HEALTH AND FITNESS (Nelson Berry)
[1325]

►SUBLIMINAL MESSAGES EXTREME (Nelson Berry)
[1326]

►SUBLIMINAL STUDIO [1327]

Those who have studied subliminal messaging believe it is powerful and effective; this is why the CIA invested millions in subliminal messaging research way back in the 1950's. The technology was expanded in the 60's following research studies by William Bryan Key, Vance Packard, and Eldon Taylor, all suggesting that subliminals are a highly effective method of influencing thought.

Subliminal messaging is a method of sending commands directly to the subconscious mind, bypassing the more critical conscious; the subconscious mind quickly absorbs and acts on these commands.

[1325] http://93af3zl6nijrmuecx9pg-fjz1l.hop.clickbank.net/
[1326] http://272c0xn6ckihtr5i460hy46od4.hop.clickbank.net/
[1327] http://www.subliminal-studio.com/?ref=48106

Anthony Robbins and Tiger Woods both claim that subliminals are the key to their success.

Ask yourself these questions ......

[1] Do you find mass produced subliminal CDs effective?

[2] Do you trust the subliminal tapes/CDs you buy?

[3] Do you sometimes want subliminal recordings for topics that most CDs do not cover?

There is a simple solution.

If you are using a Windows PC with a soundcard, then you already have all the equipment you need.

Just add the powerful *Subliminal Studio* and you will learn exactly how to create your own subliminal tapes, CDs and MP3s, virtually unheard of in the retail world.

The software CD includes: [1] *Developing Your Own Subliminal-Studio* booklet with 60 pages of exclusive information guiding you through the process of creating your own subliminal recordings, step-by-step, [2] over three hours of royalty-free relaxation music, [3] 20 pre-recorded subliminal CD scripts, [4] two and a half hours of nature sounds, also royalty free, [5] over two and a half hours of expertly created binaural beats, [6] highly sought after silent subliminal script, and [7] trial version of Adobe Audition for compiling your own subliminal recordings.

►THE INTELLIGENT WARRIOR SUBLIMINAL VIDEO SERIES (Nelson Berry) [1328]

TRILIMINALS

►QUANTUM TRILIMINALS (with TMM) [1329] [1330] [1331] [1332]

►EFFORTLESS PROSPERITY [1333] is Morry's latest, and truly amazing, program.

1328

http://d21947n2mcklumdm64rd41fubs.hop.clickbank.net/
[1329] http://www.themorrymethod.com/tmm.php?id=14
[1330] http://quantumtriliminalsuccess.com/Teleseminar2.htm
[1331] http://quantumtriliminals.com/trial.htm
[1332] http://quantum-mind-power-system.com/fp2/index.html
[1333] http://339150jaf8wnpr27iex9zn3k4e.hop.clickbank.net/

Given that one has the power to change their thoughts at any time, so, too, does this change one's outlook (viewpoint, mindset, perception, paradigm) on their reality.

This means that when you are able to change your thinking (courtesy of your brain), so, too, does it change your life. [1334]

No matter how you may be struggling to turn your current circumstances around or improve your lot in life, there *is* a powerful secret that actually changes your brain from a place of confusion, discouragement, or negativity, into a powerful vibrational force that will change your life; in fact, scientific research actually proves this to be true.

In summation, the formula to a life of prosperity (peace of mind, emotional well-being, happiness, financial freedom) and abundance is far simpler than most people can possibly imagine.

[1334] http://effortlessprosperityprogram.com/wp/ep-forgiveness/

Additional Programs Purchased

This is the section of the book whereby I highlight other programs that I have purchased, and am continuing to use successfully, but do not have an affiliate relationship with.

This does *not* mean that they are any less valuable and/or that I would not recommend them; some programs simply do not support affiliate features.

AFFIRMATIONS

▶ AFFIRM-A-LIFE MASTERCLASS [1335]

Reprogram your mindset instantly while you passively activate the power of your subsconscious mind through repetition, featuring MP3 audios for [1] Self Discovery Affirmations, [2] Goal Setting Affirmations, [3] Marketing and Business Affirmations, [4] Habits And Subconscious

---

[1335] http://www.goalzila.com/affirmalife/

Affirmations, [5] Financial Freedom Affirmations, [6] Relationships Affirmations, [7] Health And Wellness Affirmations, [8] Positive Thinking Affirmations, [9] Spirituality Affirmations, [10] Daily Affirmations to Kick Start Your Day. In addition, there are some amazing bonuses (total cost $7).

AFFORMATIONS

▶THE AFFORMATIONS BLUEPRINT: A STEP-BY-STEP FORMULA TO DESIGN THE LIFE OF YOUR DREAMS (amazing cost of $47) [1336]

Your brain is the most powerful tool you have to become more successful in life. For a great many, using affirmation statements to create the ideal life merely constitutes wishful thinking; on a subconscious level (where it really counts), our brains do not believe.

This Afformations Method, which consists primarily of four elements and employs five specific mind-penetrating techniques, allows you to quickly attract more money

---

[1336] http://www.afformations.com/letter/

through the power of your subconscious mind (where 97% of all decisions are made).

►iAFFORM AUDIO SERIES [1337]

BRAINWAVE ENTRAINMENT

►HARMONIC ASCENSION (Jody Sachse) [1338]

An exclusive (members only) spiritual self improvement website with over 30 cutting edge brainwave entrainment meditations, a packed resources section with tons of ebooks, downloads and links to other amazing resources with more being added all the time.

►MYSTIC MINDPOWER (Jody Sachse) [1339] has a wide range of unique brainwave entrainment meditations, ranging from beta, alpha, theta, delta and gamma brainwave frequencies.

[1337] http://noahstjohn.com/products/iafform-audio-afformations/
[1338] http://harmonicascension.com/
[1339] http://mysticmindpower.com/

►MYSTIC MINDPOWER EVOLUTION BRAINWAVE ENTRAINMENT MEDITATION GUIDE [1340]

HO'OPONOPONO

►Z PLUS ADVANCED HO'OPONOPONO SUBLIMINAL CLEARING [1341]

HYPNOSIS

►MINDFIT HYPNOSIS [1342] is a website that offers hypnosis (hypnotherapy) sessions based on a wide variety of topic areas. They also offer a FREE online hypnotic induction video. [1343]

►NATURAL HYPNOSIS [1344] is a website that offers natural, powerful, hypnosis CDs and MP3 audio files.

[1340] http://mysticmindpower.com/mp3/MME-Guide.pdf
[1341] http://www.subliminalclearing.com/
[1342] http://www.mindfithypnosis.com/all-hypnosis-mp3
[1343] http://www.mindfithypnosis.com/free-online-hypnosis-induction
[1344] http://www.naturalhypnosis.com/

They also offer three FREE albums so that you can see if hypnosis is right for you. [1345]

Finding the voice of Brennan Smith to be very soothing, I make use of MP3 audio files for [1] business success, [2] confidence, [3] health, [4] manifestation success, [5] mind enhancement, [6] personal development, [7] productivity and [8] success.

MANIFESTATION

►MANIFEST A MIRACLE (Gary Evans) [1346]

►THE 7 ESSENTIAL UNIVERSAL LAWS (Christy Whitman) [1347]

►THE 11 FORGOTTEN LAWS (Bob Proctor, Mary Morrissey) [1348]

[1345] http://www.naturalhypnosis.com/l/try-hypnosis-free/
[1346] http://www.manifestmiracle.com/
[1347] http://www.7essentiallaws.com/essentiallaws.php
[1348] http://www.the11forgottenlaws.com/

▶THE HIDDEN SECRET IN THINK AND GROW RICH (Brian Kim) [1349]

▶THE NEW MESSAGE OF A MASTER (Kristen Howe) [1350]

MINDFULNESS

▶UNLOCK THE POWER OF NOW (Kristen Howe) [1351]

SUBLIMINALS

▶MINDFIT HYPNOSIS [1352] is a website that offers subliminal message therapy sessions based on a wide variety of topic areas.

They also offer a FREE subliminal session entitled Live Life with Passion and Purpose, [1353] something we all need to be reminded of.

[1349] http://www.briankim.net/hiddensecret.php
[1350] http://www.newmessageofamaster.com/
[1351] http://unlockthepowerofnow.com/
[1352] http://www.mindfithypnosis.com/subliminal-mp3

►REAL SUBLIMINAL [1354] is a website that offers subliminal CDs and MP3 audio files to directly penetrate your un-conscious mind, allowing you to make lasting changes to your thoughts, habits, and behavior to dramatically improve your life, and help you to achieve your goals much easier.

►THOUGHTS INSPIRE SUBLIMINALS [1355] is a website that offers subliminal MP3 audio files that utilize BrainTune® technology.

Their subliminal messaging system uses a special combination of carefully crafted I and You affirmations which are much more effective than normal subliminal messaging alone.

The I affirmations create the effect of you believing that the new thoughts have been inspired within you naturally.

[1353] http://www.mindfithypnosis.com/live-with-passion-and-purpose-subliminal-message
[1354] http://www.realsubliminal.com/
[1355] http://www.thoughtinspire.com/products.html

The <u>You affirmations</u> provided you with external validation and approval of the changes which are taking place.

It is this multi-pronged and holistic approach which amplifies the effects of Thought Inspire™ [1356] above anything else.

You can also try out three free subliminals. [1357]

[1356] http://www.thoughtinspire.com/howitworks.html

[1357]

http://www.thoughtinspire.com/demoaudio.html?pid=nBKd VaoSPd&a_id=danb

About the Author

Michele Doucette is webmistress of Portals of Spirit, a spirituality website.

As a Level 2 Reiki Practitioner, she sends long distance Reiki to those who make the request, claiming only to be a facilitator of the Universal energy, meaning that it is up to the individual(s) in question to use these energies in order to heal themselves.

Having also acquired a Crystal Healing Practitioner diploma (Stonebridge College in the UK), she is guardian to many from the mineral kingdom.

She is the author of many spiritual/metaphysical works; namely, [1] The Ultimate Enlightenment For 2012: All We Need Is Ourselves, a book that was nominated for the AllBooks Review Best Inspirational Book of 2011, [2] Turn Off The TV: Turn On Your Mind, [3] Veracity At Its Best, [4] The Collective: Essays on Reality (a composition of essays in relation to the Matrix), [5] Sleepers Awaken: The

Time Is Now To Consciously Create Your Own Reality, [6] Healing the Planet and Ourselves: How To Raise Your Vibration, [7] You Are Everything: Everything Is You, [8] The Awakening of Humanity: A Foremost Necessity, [9] The Cosmos of The Soul: A Spiritual Biography, [10] Getting Out Of Our Own Way: Love Is The Only Answer, [11] Living The Jedi Way, [12] Vicarius Christi: The Vicar of Christ and [13] A Metaphysics Primer: Changing From The Inside Out, all of which have been published through St. Clair Publications.

In addition, she has written another volume that deals solely with crystals, aptly entitled The Wisdom of Crystals.

She is also the author of A Travel in Time to Grand Pré, a visionary metaphysical novel that historically ties the descendants of Yeshua (Jesus) to modern day Nova Scotia.

As shared by a reviewer, it is the volume Veracity At Its Best that "constructs the context for the spiritual message" imparted in A Travel in Time to Grand Pré.

Against the backdrop of 1754 Acadie, this novel, an alchemical tale of time travel, romance and intrigue, from Henry Sinclair to the Merovingians, from the Cathari treasure at Montségur to the Knights Templar, also blends French Acadian history with current DNA testing.

Together with the words of Yeshua as spoken at the height of his ministry, A Travel in Time to Grand Pré has the potential to inspire others; for it is herein that we learn how individuals can find their way, their truth(s), so as to live their lives to the fullest.

Several years in the making, she was also driven to write Back Home With Evangeline, the sequel to A Travel in Time to Grand Pré.

It is here that Madeleine and Michel find themselves back in the twentieth century with a message that must be shared with the world. So, too, and even more importantly, must the message be lived, and experienced, by one and all.

So, too, is she the author of <u>Time Will Tell</u>, a uniquely moving tale that begins in the present day before weaving its way backward through time to connect a glowing thread of historic discoveries.

Courtesy of past-life regression, Michaela (Dr. Mike) Callaghan, a brilliant metaphysical scientist, in the twenty-first century, discovers that she lived as a young, noble, Cathari herbalist healer, in the Languedoc area of France, during a time when political change was in the air.

When not working as a Special Education teacher, she continues to read, research and write, exploring her personal genealogies, all of which constitute her passion.

In the words of the Dalai Lama … *In order to be happy, one must first possess inner contentment; and inner contentment cannot come from having all we want; rather it comes from having and appreciating all we have.*

www.ingramcontent.com/pod-product-compliance
Lightning Source LLC
Chambersburg PA
CBHW060449090426
42735CB00011B/1955